Ed —

Merry

Christmas

Love,

Patti ♡

A CRAFTSMAN'S LEGACY

A CRAFTSMAN'S LEGACY

Why Working with Our Hands
Gives Us Meaning

ERIC GORGES

with Jon Sternfeld

ALGONQUIN BOOKS
OF CHAPEL HILL
2019

Published by
Algonquin Books of Chapel Hill
Post Office Box 2225
Chapel Hill, North Carolina 27515-2225

a division of
Workman Publishing
225 Varick Street
New York, New York 10014

LIBRARY OF CONGRESS CATALOGING-IN-PUBLICATION DATA

Names: Gorges, Eric, author.
Title: A craftsman's legacy : why working with our
hands gives us meaning / Eric Gorges.
Description: Chapel Hill, North Carolina : Algonquin Books of
Chapel Hill, [2019] | Includes bibliographical references.
Identifiers: LCCN 2018042246 | ISBN 9781616208363 (hardcover : alk. paper)
Subjects: LCSH: Handicraft—Philosophy.
Classification: LCC TT149 .G575 2019 | DDC 745.5—dc23
LC record available at https://lccn.loc.gov/2018042246

10 9 8 7 6 5 4 3 2 1
First Edition

CONTENTS

A CRAFTSMAN'S LEGACY

INTRODUCTION: FROM OUR HANDS

We find only one tool, neither created nor invented, but perfect: the hand of man. —JULIO RAMÓN RIBEYRO

I build custom motorcycles for a living, so as a craftsman, I work with a variety of materials, tools, and machines. But my primary tools will always be my hands. And, to be honest, mine have been through the grinder.

Any dreams of becoming a famous hand model have burned to the ground. My thumb is currently an alarming shade of black—smashed from having two pounds of metal dead dropped on it. My hands bleed all the time, their skin is rough and cracked like a dirt road, and there's a gnarly scar across my right index knuckle. I have scars on my hands that go back years, injuries whose sources have been lost to my memory.

I think of them all as badges of honor. My hands are beat up from *use*. Hands tell a story, so it seems fitting then that when we greet someone, we shake hands. It's personal and intimate; it allows us to identify ourselves to each other and exchange information. For craftsmen, especially, our hands are often the extension of our desires and our vision. They are how we create, repair, and make an impact on the world.

It's why the idea of something being handmade is special. As mass production makes everything transitional and disposable, the personal object becomes even more valuable. I think about my grandparents going to buy furniture seventy years ago. Back then, it would have been a big decision, an *event*. They would have likely bought one piece of furniture at a time—a table, a dresser, a sofa—and that piece would be built to last, maybe for fifty years. They assumed their grandchildren would sit on that sofa one day. Nowadays, because of the convenience, we're often buying things from a picture on the Internet. Our connection to the object is virtual, really an illusion. I believe we need to be able to touch something to truly know it. Ordinarily, the first thing I like to do before I buy furniture is the shake test; it's an automatic thing, literally shaking the object. I get a look at the piece, a feel of the joinery, a sense of how it is all assembled. I want to know if it'll last or if I'm going to be back in the store next year.

Some months back I found myself on a Saturday afternoon staring at a few boxes. My girlfriend and I had recently broken up, and I had moved out and needed furniture. I work with my hands for a living, and I produce and host a show about the value of working with your hands, where I meet other people who work with *their* hands, but time and money were tight. So I did what most people do: I logged on to my computer and picked out a new couch online. Though I'd eventually want furniture that would last, I needed something right away that would fit my current life situation. I had a short timeline and nowhere to sit.

A few days later, three different boxes showed up at my front door. I was looking at them with my daughter, trying to figure out what was in there. Was this my sofa? Split into three boxes? In one box was the couch's bottom. We unzipped it to find all the cushions packed inside, and then the other pieces, which were to be bolted together. That couch served a purpose, but it was never going to last long enough to be passed down to my daughter.

IN THE TWENTY-FIRST century, we've become passive figures in the larger churning machine, further removed from how things are made, how they work, the people who made them, and how the dots all connect. As we've become distant from the rest of the world we have become more and more distant from each other. In some ways, we've become distant from *ourselves*. That's why I'm on a mission to celebrate craftsmanship.

This book features craftsmen, their work, and their way of life. Craftsmen were once the backbone of our country, but they have been pushed to the margins. Just like the things they make, however, they are resilient. On *A Craftsman's Legacy*, craftsmen invite me into their homes and shops, and I try what they do myself, right there in front of the camera.

It's been wonderful to see the recent resurgence of handmade items, and I'm optimistic that will continue to expand the appreciation of and interest in craftsmanship. But we can all learn and be inspired through the spirit of craftsmen and their work, whether or not we make things ourselves. The lessons discussed here are universal. Maybe an understanding of the craftsman's ethic can help someone feel more grounded in their own life or bring the wisdom of the natural and mechanical worlds back into our homes, offices, and day-to-day existences.

In my estimation, craftsmen are heroic to me, and I'm trying to do the little bit I can to shine the light back on them.

—ERIC GORGES
Detroit, Michigan

1: THE BATTLE FOR PERFECTION

We are what we repeatedly do. Excellence, then, is not an act, but a habit. —ARISTOTLE

The first ten thousand pots are difficult. Then it gets a little bit easier. —WARREN MACKENZIE, *potter*

Every time you get in the saddle, you are up against the impossible. No matter your years of experience or level of expertise, this is an immutable truth. There's probably nothing more necessary in craftsmanship than accepting this fact. In the introduction to every episode of *A Craftsman's Legacy* I say that the craftsman "battles" for perfection. I use that word consciously because it *is* a battle; it's a messy and valiant struggle that each one of us is bound to lose.

In accepting imperfection I am in good company, joining a long tradition that is practiced in cultures around the world. A Japanese aesthetic called *wabi-sabi* embraces the imperfect, and in Zen Buddhist tea ceremonies, the pots and cups have intentional irregularities in them. Orthodox Jews insist on putting a flaw in every house they construct as a reminder of their lost holy temple. The Navajo traditionally insert mistakes in their rugs because that's where "the soul moves in and out of the rug." Islamic culture does the same thing with Persian rugs, as a testament to the fact that only God can make perfection.

Human beings simply cannot create perfection with our hands. We can make things eye-perfect, but measurements will never lie. An object made by hand will have that human stamp on it. That's what gives a piece its soul. Rather than turn away from this reality, various cultures have decided to lean in to this fact.

None of this means I have thrown in the towel. I still chase perfection in my work every day, trying to get as close as I can. But my history is littered with countless items I've destroyed in a vain effort to make them flawless. In my office at Voodoo Choppers, my motorcycle shop, I still have the first ever motorcycle fuel tank I made—or rather, *tried* to make. I spent so much time finishing the side in an effort to get it exactly right that I chewed right through the metal.

All of that extra effort was ignoring the obvious: It was never good enough to begin with. I thought if I pushed enough through failure I'd come out the other end with a fuel tank. What I ended up with was a hole. So I enlarged the gap and shaped it into an oval, and today it sits in my office holding brochures. It's a good reminder of the impossibility of perfection.

I was younger then and didn't yet know what I know now: To win the war you have to accept loss in the battle. At some point you stop learning from a piece and are just going through the motions. The trick is in knowing when it's time to walk away from it. At first it's hard to get there because you have to overcome your pride. But with age and experience, we start to let go of those unattainable visions for our work—and for ourselves.

It's a tension all craftsmen deal with. Like knife maker Tim Zowada said to me, "I haven't made a perfect one yet." That *yet* sums up the contradiction. He knows he can't—but he's still holding on to an inkling of hope. It's the chase that motivates us, though I don't think anyone thinks they're going to catch that car.

Craftsmen live and work at the mercy of these contradicting ideas—serving the past and future, possessing confidence and humility, honoring the simple and the complex, having control and submitting to the mystery. It's the raw heaviness of work, like wailing on metal with hammers and stoking coal into the fire. It's churning machines and noise and sparks. But it's also inches and details. It's dexterity and delicacy. It's persistence, working your tail off on something day and night and then just . . . letting it be.

"You've got to start losing interest in a piece as soon as it's done," wood turner Alan Hollar told me. "You've got to have more interest in the one you're going to do than in the one you just did. Or you just stay in the same place all the time." That commitment to forward progression—to the next piece—is the kind of wisdom that comes from years in the saddle. You're fighting against the constraints of time, life, business—and you're never going to win. You're not meant to. That's frustrating, but it's also beautiful. The struggle keeps you growing. It gives us all a little kick, an extra engine. That's something we can all use to become our best selves. That's why I keep up the fight.

It is my charge to always improve upon it into the future.
—JAKE WEIDMANN, *master penman*

JAKE WEIDMANN IS one of only of twelve people in the world—and the youngest in history—with his title: master penman. It's a royal-sounding title, and he's got the proof, which, of course, he designed himself. The final test for his calligraphy training was to make his own certificate, which is a document of incomparable beauty.

As a boy Jake was inspired by his mother's gorgeous script. Once he learned cursive, he began to dazzle his teachers with his artistic and fluid writing. Art seemed to naturally spring from his hands, and people noticed. Professors in school would ask to keep his assignments, even his class *notes*, because of the care and beauty of his penmanship. It would be like listening to a tape of John Coltrane playing scales or tasting a casual lunch that Julia Child made for herself.

Jake practices calligraphy, the decorative handwriting style with a long tradition, but he also draws, paints, and carves wood, including making his own tools. The designing came out of necessity. He couldn't find a pen that worked the way he needed it to—the way he envisioned it *should*—so he created his own. This led to a series of exquisite pens that Jake designed, out of wood, animal bone, and stone. The calligraphy pen has to capture the complicated inner mind of the artist, so according to Jake, "it should be a tool worthy of the task."

I had been hearing about Jake's work for a while and knew I wanted to book him on *A Craftsman's Legacy*. He's a spiritual guy, a romantic at heart, who lives near the Colorado Rocky Mountains, which no photograph has ever done justice.

Jake has a singular way of carrying himself, and he speaks in this careful way that echoes his writing. It's a hyperarticulate and elevated manner of talking that reminded me of a poet or a knight, like a man from another time.

I don't know if he's like this because of his lettering work or if he was attracted to lettering because of this aspect of his personality, but it doesn't really matter. Who he is and what he does are inseparable. He's wholly committed to his craft and, by extension, his vision of the world. Every craftsman has one—whether consciously or not—which they express through their work.

I asked Jake my standard question, something I ask every guest on the show: Do you consider yourself an artist or a craftsman? The idea of it interests me, where the lines are, how blurred they are, how self-perception and self-identity play a role in their work. The answers are so revealing.

Sometimes the guest has clearly thought about these two terms and feels they are a craftsman. Others negotiate an answer that's somewhere in the middle. Other times, the question seems irrelevant to them and they tell me they haven't thought much about it, like the name is beside the point. The more I ask that question the more I realize the label has more to do with how the person feels about his work than anything technical or inherent in the work itself.

Jake's answer was as thoughtful and distinct as any I had heard. "He who works with his hands is a laborer," he quoted. "He who works with his hands and his head is a craftsman. He who works with his hands and his head and his heart is an artist." He didn't say it outright, but I think it's clear he views himself an artist.

Handwriting is a representation of our selves that is fading from society. Script has vanished from the classroom and penmanship is no longer emphasized. The assumption is that kids can pick it up on their own time or they don't really need to master it because they communicate through computers. But something is getting lost: What's more personal than your handwriting? It practically carries your DNA. Forensic experts can evaluate signatures and read your fears and desires from the way you curl your *g*. The reason it's so valuable is because our true nature—the selves we can hide in other ways—comes through in our handwriting. It tells the world something about us that we might not want to share. Maybe something we don't even know.

Back when all writing was done by hand, texts were works of art, venerated like sculpture or painting. Think about the

Declaration of Independence or the U.S. Constitution and the beautiful flowing script we associate with those documents. When we look at them today we can still picture Thomas Jefferson and James Madison sitting down, dipping a pen into an inkwell, and bringing their words to life. Everything from the paper those documents are written on to the curl and swirl of the letters to the words themselves communicates their higher purpose. They are pieces of paper worthy of building a country from or swearing an oath to.

If you ever get a chance to look at letters from Revolutionary or Civil War soldiers writing home, stop and look closely. They are incredible. Likely they were exhausted, wet, injured, terrified, and dirty, and yet so many of their letters are written in this flowing, beautiful script. It shows so clearly how valued writing used to be. They were communicating to their loved ones, and their writing—not just the words, but the actual *writing*—expressed how they felt.

My cousin once gave me a letter that my grandfather wrote while he was fighting in World War II. It was on U.S. Army stationery and preserved in a plastic sheath. I was mesmerized when I first took hold of it, and that feeling hasn't worn off. Something about that letter felt so alive; it is an authentic record of my history, my family's history, and the country's history. It connects me to my grandfather and his life, his era and place, his loves and fears and desires and struggles. Through his letter—through his handwriting—I can enter his world. In that way, the physical act of writing is like a portal through time and space.

. . .

Two thousand years ago the Romans invented the reed pen, which was made from either reed or bamboo. It remained the most popular writing device in the Western world for over five hundred years, until the quill, made from bird feathers, was invented in Spain sometime in the sixth century. Handwritten text was the only option for nearly a thousand years—and the low literacy rate meant it was practiced by a select few. That was the status quo until Germany's Johannes Gutenberg invented the printing press with movable type around 1440, which prompted the spread of books and reading. With the increasing mechanization of writing, along with the rise of the fountain pen in the eighteenth century, which didn't require dipping, the craft of lettering and calligraphy fell into decline.

English translator William Morris resurrected the calligraphy arts during the Arts and Crafts movement of the late nineteenth century, which itself was a reaction to the industrialization of modern life. Morris obsessively studied medieval and Renaissance texts to learn various writing styles. The modern calligraphy tradition, which Jake Weidmann proudly helps to carry on, extends down from there.

Calligraphy—a combining of two Greek words, one for "beautiful" and one for "writing"—both preserves an individual's personal writing style and elevates it to an art form. Ironically, or maybe fittingly, it was a calligraphy class that Steve Jobs took in college that gave him the idea of giving Apple computers "beautiful typography." He wanted to bring that real-world aesthetic to the zeros and ones of the computer.

Even executing a simple letter in calligraphy takes great patience and skill. Jake uses a dip (or nib) pen with an exquisite wood or bone holder that he has to continually dip into an ink reservoir on his desk. The nib at the end of the pen is split into two tines, like a fork, which collect the ink. When you are writing, you are applying pressure, which causes the tines to spread, and it is this spreading that creates different line styles and thickness. Learning to master how much pressure to apply, the direction of the pen and nib, and how much ink gets used are just a few of the factors that make calligraphy challenging.

Calligraphy is closer to painting than common writing in that subtle movements heavily impact the final product. Unlike regular writing, the amount of pressure applied from pen to paper varies: for instance, downward strokes require a harder press than upward ones. One of the strokes Jake taught me was like a wave or a snake. It is known as the "universal line of beauty," a term coined by painter and critic William Hogarth in the eighteenth century. It appears in nature and art with high frequency, and the name itself strikes me as so grand—it captures the artist's higher purpose and the interconnectedness of living things, how there's a shared ethos across all of them.

Spending time with someone like Jake is enough to make you believe that society's current emphasis on being well-rounded is misguided. He is committed to doing the single task well, and he's a great advertisement for it. He is centered and passionate and extraordinarily talented. Getting something right—not perfect, but *right*—takes time and patience and an almost obsessive attention to detail. Because Jake's efforts are directed to a single point, he has reached a rare level of his craft.

Jake is not just keeping the craft and tradition alive, as though it were an inert thing reluctantly being dragged forward; he's breathing new life into it so it can stand on its own, move ahead on its own strength. On his website, he writes: "You cannot honor the past by repeating it. You honor the past by giving it new life and relevance in our modern age." He has such a deep, almost mystical understanding of his purpose that I was inspired being around him.

"We live in a world of quick and easy, and so things fade away just as quickly," Jake told me. "To have something that has permanence on that page is so beautiful." He and his wife—who is also an artist—have kept all their letters to each other. One day, they would like to pass them down to their children and grandchildren, so the story of them falling in love will live on—through their written words.

When I came back home to Michigan after spending time with Jake, I had a whole new appreciation of and outlook on my handwriting. I practiced calligraphy strokes and even started writing all my communications by hand, which I still try to do. The effect it had on me was profound. I now take the time to slow down and think about how I am corresponding. Friends of mine who receive my letters say they appreciate them, how it feels so much better than a text or email. I think maybe it's because the letter wasn't only a vehicle for what I wanted to convey—the physical paper and writing itself communicated the time and care I felt my friends deserved.

My handwriting actually has been horrible for as long as I remember, but it's only because I hadn't taken the time to learn this skill. Now, I make it a habit to practice. Lately I've been using cursive even for day-to-day things like checks, envelopes, and notes. It takes a little more time, but it *should*. And maybe if we took more time when sharing our thoughts, we'd avoid the problems that no doubt arise from quick and distracted communication. I'm not sure, but it seems possible.

As I rediscovered the written word I started realizing how strange it is that emojis are so popular now. It's funny— in a sense we're working our way back to communicating with pictures again, which is where we started, with cave paintings and hieroglyphics. Only this time the pictures don't even have the personal stamp; they're standardized for convenience and time. As I try to be more conscious about what I'm writing, my hope is that it will spill over into other parts of my life.

JAKE HAS REACHED the apex of his profession, and despite his talent, the journey along the way has not been a straight line. In order to take your skills to the next level, in anything, you have to push. As you keep climbing rungs, learning a harder set of skills, the amount of time you put in increases as well. They're proportional. That's why there are so few who are really great at what they do; people drop out along the way. To become great at anything, you have to persist past the point where you even know what you're doing. It's stepping onto a bridge that you haven't built yet.

As a professional I never lose that desire to learn and the sense that I need to. I try to go into every project with that level of perspective: *What can I learn from this?*

The battle for perfection always entails a healthy dose of failure. And it's not just failure but an acceptance, even an embrace, of that failure. I fail all the time, and I try to use it as a tool: for growth, for learning, for excellence. If I think back on my life and my work, I've never really gotten anywhere by staying in my comfort zone. The failure is the thing that has continually pushed me forward and outward.

By stepping into that battle, by embracing the purpose of the battle itself, I try to keep the independent spirit alive. I think anyone who makes something for a living, whatever it is, is putting part of themselves into their work, making a commitment to doing something right, and celebrating the work's humanness instead of hiding its flaws. They're not flaws at all. The flaw is in thinking we can make something without any.

2: TEARING UP FLOORS

I'm twelve years old and it's Friday night. My younger brother, Scott, and I are watching *CHiPs*, waiting for *The Dukes of Hazzard* to come on. At the end of the couch, my dad is lost in his own world, stewing as he stares at the living room carpeting—almost *into* the living room carpeting. This is normal: Dad is almost always stewing about something. My brother and I know better than to set him off.

Out of the corner of my eye, I see my dad lean forward, his hands reaching outward. Then he gets up and eagerly grabs an end of the carpet and starts lifting, and it tears, the *rita-tick-tick* of the seams separating. I briefly catch the look on his face and can see his tired eyes opening wide, the wheels spinning in his head. "Jesus," he says, to no one in particular, "there's parquet under here."

Scottie and I don't move. We don't look over.

"Hey! Guys, get over here," my dad says. There's a pause— *Maybe it'll pass*, I think. *The Dukes of Hazzard* is just about to start. "Eric! Scott! Get over here!"

I silently groan as Scottie and I walk away from the TV. I look up but can only see the side of the television from here. My dad is kneeling on the floor, messing with his new discovery. I know where this is headed. I've seen *this* show before.

THAT'S USUALLY HOW it started at my house. Once Dad got going there was nothing to stop him. A question, an observation, maybe a strange noise and then we were knee-deep into it—spending the rest of the night on one project or another. That particular night was spent stripping up the living room carpet, cutting it, rolling it, then tying it, and carrying it out to the trash. Afterward we had to pull up all the pieces of the broken wood underneath.

At some point in the middle of all this my mom walked in and saw us covered in dust, the room in absolute shambles. "What the hell is going on?" she asked. "What are you guys doing?" The project lasted about month or two—we reset all the wood squares by hand and replaced the unsalvageable ones. By the time it was all done the parquet floor was beautiful. I couldn't deny it: My dad was right.

Growing up, my house was a boot camp for learning how to build and fix things. I never heard, "You're too young, don't touch that." If it needed to be done, I was asked to do it. Early on, I got used to the idea that there were no barriers to what people can do. As a kid I didn't appreciate it—I just thought my dad was a pain in the ass—but I'm not sure I'd be where I am without that experience and confidence.

My dad was an all-around, hands-on guy. I can't ever remember seeing a tradesman at our house, even though there were major projects going on all the time—laying down floors, masonry work, putting in windows, cement work, building this, demoing that, repairing something else. When something broke, we fixed it. When something was needed, we built it. It allowed me to learn a lot at a very young age; more importantly, it made me fearless about making mistakes. And that spirit has stuck with me.

I can remember being about six years old and going downstairs with my dad to the basement. While he worked on remodeling down there, installing a wet bar and built-in cabinets, he'd give me a hammer, some nails, and pieces of wood and just let me be. So I'd sit on the floor and run nails into two-by-fours and make funny shapes, create something out of whatever he let me use. Later on I got a tool belt and excitedly filled it up with nails, tape, pliers, and a hammer. It was all play—playing at doing work.

As I got older, and less resentful of being put to work, I'd stand beside or behind my dad on a project and try to help. Sometimes I'd get the chance and make a mess or break something, which made him pretty upset, but never enough that it curbed my willingness to get in there and figure it out. I knew that on the other side of that mistake was something new to discover.

I WENT TO Catholic school, a place with strict rules and stern teachers who had no tolerance for my antics. I didn't care enough to apply myself, so my grades were always subpar. Socializing wasn't my thing either; I had a couple of friends, but I was always afraid of looking foolish, so I tended to keep to myself. Sports were the main currency, and I wasn't coordinated enough to excel at any of them. Plus, I didn't have the time or opportunity to get good, because I was usually working. Not that I really minded.

My family started a lawn fertilizing company when I was young, and our house was basically home base. There were always employees and vehicles coming and going, trucks that needed loading or maintenance, machinery that needed fixing. A couple of times a year I would go door to door to hand out flyers, which my dad printed himself. He knew absolutely nothing about printing except that it'd be significantly cheaper (and easier to change and update) if he did it on his own. So he figured it out. He purchased printing equipment and set up an offset press in the basement. It was the full deal: single head offset press, camera, folding machine, cutter.

What seeped into my young mind was my dad's fearlessness about figuring how what he needed to learn and then learning it. We had sets of *Time* books in the house that taught you how to do anything—framing, electrical work, painting—so everything seemed possible. My father embraced that openness; there was absolutely nothing he was afraid to try.

That business eventually grew into a nursery, where I worked on weekends. I didn't feel like I was missing out by having to be there because I dug it. I got to wear work boots and leather gloves, and I was splitting and stacking firewood in the winter, cutting up wood on the hydraulic splitter or with a chain saw, dragging trees and shrubs out to customers' cars in the summer. Childhood is our first lens into reality, and that was mine.

My dad had a three-piece stack of toolboxes and a set of oxy acetylene tanks and torches. I was captivated by welding, but those tools were the only ones off-limits to me. To my young mind, the idea of being able to join metal seemed like something only a superhero could do. Even the mask with the lid was badass. I must've asked my dad a thousand times to teach me how to use the torch, but I never got anywhere. That withholding did nothing but build up my desire to get my hands on one. I could see myself in the future, dropping that lid and bringing that flame into a piece of metal. Nothing fascinated me more.

3: FOCUS

Creative fulfillment is not something to achieve and keep, like a college degree or an Olympic medal. It resides in the process of making the table, not in the satisfaction of sitting at it. —PETER KORN, *furniture maker*

If I can help it, I try not to give time estimates for work I'm doing at Voodoo Choppers. It wouldn't make any sense: I don't know how long something will take until I get into the job. Almost all craftsmen face this reality—when asked how long something will take, we all say some version of the same thing: *It takes as long as it takes.*

I don't say it out of ego or to be a jerk; I just literally have no idea. When I've tried in the past to project timelines I've been so wildly off that I've learned it's better to not even pretend. I'm open and honest with my customers, but

I know the work suffers when it's dictated by an arbitrary schedule. We're bringing things to life in there. *Breathing* life into them.

As a business owner it is one of those things I continually struggle with. I'd like to be able to get things done in a timely way, but making it right, being proud of the final product, that's the priority. It pushes all other concerns to the margins. That's not to say I don't hustle to get things done when necessary. I'm not immune to schedules and to-do lists, but I made a decision some time ago not to let them run me.

To actually get into the shop and build something, I have to shut everything else out. I have to get lost in there. Excellence requires staying in the present moment, concentrating on what's in front of me right now, condensing and contracting the world down to a size where I can control it. It requires focus.

Focus is essentially concentration and drive. My mind is filled with the same chatter of regular worries as everyone's: *Did I pay the utility bill?* Can *I pay the utility bill? Is my kid excelling in school? Is my relationship going well?* It's a constant tug-of-war, but I make a conscious decision, when my mind wanders, just to ease myself back. The best way is to remind myself that I have to make a decision: *Do I care enough about what I'm doing to not let other things get in the way?* It's like how a camera cannot focus the entire frame; some of the frame has to be blurry in order to sharpen the object you're shooting.

So day-to-day worries knock at my door and I choose not to get up to answer. The rest of the world starts at the forefront of my head, and then it dissolves, into noise, then white noise, and then—silence. Then it's time to really get down to work.

Maybe we're destined for things. Maybe there's a book where the script is all written out for us and we just have to be aware enough to notice when we've encountered something of importance.
—DAVID MACDONALD, *potter*

DAVID MACDONALD IS a potter in Syracuse, New York, far upstate near the Great Lakes. With his graying beard and wire-rimmed glasses, he looks like he's been teaching college for forty-plus years, which he has. Low-key and intelligent, he is unassuming in manner but substantial in presence. There's this grounded confidence that comes through when he speaks that sounds a lot like wisdom.

While studying painting as an undergraduate, David grew tired of bringing his work home to his parents and facing their perplexed looks: *What does it mean? Which side is up?* Majoring in arts education, he found himself in a required pottery course where the first assignment was to make a cup. A few days later, on the way to another class, he swung by the shop, curious to see how it had turned out. The professor was just then unloading the kiln and told David his cup was good, at least for a beginner. He suggested David use it to drink coffee when staying up late for exams.

David couldn't wait; he cut his next class, brought his creation back to the dorm, and made some instant coffee. As he brought the cup to his lips, it was like a switch had been flipped on. The circuits lit up in his mind. What was once a lump of dirt was now *this*. This thing he could see and hold and drink out of. He wanted to chase that feeling, experience it again and again. Flawed as the cup was, David had an intimate connection, something he hadn't had with any of his paintings. That he hadn't had with anything else in his life.

David was hooked by both the beauty and the utilitarian nature of pottery. Though pottery is used decoratively, unlike a painting, that's not its purpose. It's a vessel, and we have a different relationship with a vessel than we do with a strict piece of art. There's a *tangible* give-and-take. When David started bringing his pieces home to his parents, they never needed to ask what they were for. Pottery speaks a universal language.

THE TERM "POTTERY" actually refers to any object of earth material that is then heated to become something else, so it includes glass and ceramics. It is one of the oldest crafts there is, going back twenty-five thousand years by some estimates. Pitchers for carrying food and water were developed around 10,000 B.C. The potter's wheel, which originally required hand-turning, was likely first invented by the Sumerians in Mesopotamia around 3000 B.C. Once the foot pedal was introduced, the potter was free to use both hands for shaping. This invention was instrumental in the development of ceramics as both a craft and an art form.

Pottery has been invaluable to historians and archeologists because time doesn't wipe it away. Though the full piece may break, its remains stuck around long after the people— or even whole civilizations—have passed or moved on. Over time the pottery becomes a civilization's calling card, telling future generations about the culture, routines, and belief systems of the people who made and used it.

When David began, most contemporary pottery was influenced by Asian ceramics, and like most students then, that's where he started. But as an African American learning his craft in the 1960s, David was living at the crossroads of history. He was caught up in the civil rights movement and the political unrest that characterized that era. The emotions it sparked and the issues it raised seeped—and then flooded— into his work.

David decided that his pottery should reflect who he was, what he believed, and what he was living through. His pieces became political, often decorated with black faces and the militant symbolism of the time. These were charged pieces, influenced by Black Panther activists and African American musicians and poets. The products of a raw and righteous anger, David's art spoke to the emotions and conflicts of being an African American man in America.

These early pieces were loud and physically very large— some vessels weighed fifty pounds and were up to six feet tall. David tells me now, "I didn't know enough to know back then what I was trying to do was crazy." As he matured, he began to turn away from that confrontational style and became less enamored by big and loud pieces. "I was eating myself up from the inside out," he admitted, "trying to hold on to this anger." He simply couldn't sustain working at that fevered pitch. Letting that go led to a transformation.

David began embracing the intimacy of smaller pieces—pots, plates, and vases—things people could use and hold in their hands. It was a return to the original passion that he had discovered over that first cup he made as an undergraduate. Whereas his work once announced itself, announced himself to the world, now he's more interested in connecting with others. It seems like a natural progression. With age we often close ranks in one way or another, and making our mark becomes less about yelling loudly and more like speaking carefully. We strip away some of the excess that characterizes our youth. We *focus*.

For a new muse, David looked backward, finding inspiration in the tradition and heritage of his African ancestry. When I spoke to him, he compared his goal to that of a writer—he who spends a lifetime figuring out how to communicate in as few words as possible.

DAVID CAME INTO my life at an auspicious moment. At the time we were shooting his episode, I was going through a period of emotional turmoil. My mom, with whom I was very close, had just passed away. We buried her, and then two days later I had to travel out to Syracuse at a time when I really didn't want to leave town or talk to anybody.

The experience of losing my mother was incredibly fresh, and being on television made it especially tough. There I was in David's workshop in front of cameras and lights and sound equipment and I had to find a way to get through it. And I would get far more than that.

I had never touched a potter's wheel before in my life. With pottery, your primary tools are your hands, which actually makes it more difficult. There's no distance, and no room for error, because your body is directly interacting with the material. When I was first "throwing" alongside David, manipulating the clay on the wheel, a chunk of my clay popped off and landed on the floor with a splat. When I picked it up and tried to slam it back on, David chuckled. *That's not how it works*, his face said.

Potters can manipulate their materials in a way that's like Doctor Strange or a type of witchcraft. But of course the reality is simpler: They learn their skills and put in the seat time, and the action becomes a continuation of their bodies. At the potter's wheel, there are so many variables invisible to the naked eye, like a particular hand position or angle or a shift of weight that a professional has mastered. I was in the dark, so I started where I usually start: with their hands.

Whenever I'm watching craftsmen, I always pay attention to where they're putting their hands and if they're using a lot of pressure or holding an object lightly. Sometimes you can tell by the grip they're using or the way their skin crunches up or how the tone of their fingers changes. As my wheel spun, I kept my eye on David's hands as he worked right alongside me. But they were covered in clay, and without that reference point, I was lost. I might as well have closed my eyes.

With the wheel, everything for me was at a high speed and hard to contain. It was clear from David's control and focus that, for him, everything slowed down. David could see I was struggling. He reached over and put both of his hands on top of my hands, almost transferring his energy to my body. And it was *boom*. Instantly, I knew how much pressure to apply. With the help of his framing gesture, I was able to hold a shape. Everything suddenly made sense.

What I had made when I finished wasn't great by any means, but it did look like a bowl. I told him I was surprised as I held it up. "You're not as surprised as I am," he deadpanned. By the time we finished, I was so enamored of the process that I didn't want to stop. That's the nature of the show; often, I want to continue learning and trying, but we have to pack up and move on. But the crew had more to shoot without me in David's studio, so I asked them to pick up one of the wheels and move it to the side, and I kept working. I was over there for hours, just lost in my own world, making bowls.

It was exactly what I needed. Turns out that after my mother's death I didn't need to stay home and let my thoughts wander; I needed something to focus on, something difficult that required my full attention. In the corner of that shop in upstate New York, the entire world telescoped to that wheel and that clay.

. . .

WHEN DAVID WAS younger, he was a long-distance runner, and I think there's a line connecting his former sport and his current work: They both require that combination of gradual forward movement and intense patience. One of the things David taught his students is that when you're first trying to control a lump of rotating clay everything speeds up, but you have to learn to slow down. He didn't mean this literally—the wheel moves as it moves—but you need to *slow down the speed in yourself.* Our instinct is to speed up when something new and strange is coming at us, but our reaction should be the opposite.

Once I gave up trying to catch up and instead worked on slowing myself down, I locked into focus. I suspect it's similar to how major-league hitters see the ball moving much slower than you and I do. Their mind has catalogued all the subtleties that we don't notice. They're not intimidated by a flash of white speeding at them, because they don't see what we see. Or rather, they see *more* than we see.

I wrote David afterward to thank him for how much he had done for me, how he had given me exactly what I needed by being generous with his materials, his time, and his knowledge. He insisted that it was the clay, that he knows how therapeutic the process can be and how seductive the rhythm of the wheel is. After the show aired, so many people wrote to ask him if it was TV magic, an illusion: how I was totally lost when I sat down and then in an instant got it enough to make a bowl. He assured them it was real.

I think there is something inherent about pottery that had such a profound impact on me that day. Psychologically I was more connected because literally—physically—I was touching and shaping the material. I could see it and *feel* it. As a metal shaper, I have a barrier, a mediator I have to use, like a hammer or an English wheel. With pottery, the material flowed through my hands, and anything I did had a clear and visible result. The entire process struck me as a metaphor for life. The spinning is a constant, and it's up to the person to make an impact through an intentional and careful touch.

David considers himself a potter, as opposed to a ceramic artist, because he primarily makes vessels, which have been part of the human experience since civilization began. Once people figured out how to take dirt and clay and turn it into something permanent, we made containers to hold and carry things. Talking with David, I thought about how we're created in a vessel (a womb) and we spend our lives moving around and living in vessels.

And then we end up in one.

The wife of a friend recently asked David to make a funerary urn for her husband's ashes. This friend once collected a good deal of David's work, and now David was making a final vessel for him, one to house his remains for eternity. Reflecting on death's inevitability, David said, "We're all penciled in."

David was the spark that ignited this dormant energy within me. Though I came from a different background than he did—culturally, geographically, generationally, and in terms of my craft—and was dealing with my own personal issues, it didn't matter. In David's shop and with his encouraging presence, I was able to find a space amid his crafts and his tools where I could focus in a way that was ultimately healing. I became my own restoration project.

I ONCE THOUGHT I was an incredible multitasker. Like a lot of people, I had no idea I was working against myself, doing an injustice to my work. It's a facet, some would argue a necessity, of modern life. Who doesn't want to save time by doing two things at once? But when we multitask we're not actually doing two things at once. We're switching *back and forth* between two things. And as we do that, we're losing the flow that comes from having singular focus. The leftover attention from the previous task—the residue—carries over to the other task. So we're doing each task poorly, and it takes our minds longer to get into the flow of our task each time we return to it. When we lose focus, everything becomes a distraction; each task becomes nothing more than an obstacle to the next. The present is all we ever have, and I don't want to live life resenting it or pushing it out of my way.

When we tap into that kind of singular focus, that's when we open ourselves to moments of inspiration. These don't actually come out of nowhere; they come from years and years of working at your craft. One day the feeling gets lit, but it needs a pile of dried wood to become that raging fire. Athletes often call reaching that headspace being "in the zone." Scientists call it a "flow state," and some people claim it's actually a source of true happiness.

And I think it's true that we are happiest when we are engaged. When we are at one with what we're doing, not thinking about past or future but wholly present. I'm always seeking that feeling of losing myself in time. The irony is that when I'm in it, I don't realize it. It's only when it's over and the spell is broken that I recognize where I had been. Being so focused that I look up and all of a sudden it's four o'clock. That's my perfect day.

4: FORETHOUGHT

Making is thinking. —RICHARD SENNETT,
sociology professor and author of The Craftsman

It may not be a surprise, considering what I ended up doing for a living, but as a kid I loved building model cars and airplanes. The older I got, the more complicated they became, and I strayed from the basic, by-the-numbers type of kits. Some models gave you the option to build different versions of the same car, and then I'd take those extra parts and use them on other models. As my skills became more refined, I found my way into new challenges, sanding the molded pieces to reduce joints, painting details, or using thread to look like spark plug wires.

Even as I became proficient at the models, the one part I always had trouble with was waiting for the glue to dry. I was so eager to move on to the next phase, to see what it looked like all put together. Inevitably the final piece would have mistakes—some minor, some not so minor. I was a kid, so I didn't think ahead to how skipping steps was going to come back and bite me. I was also too young to realize the bigger issue at work: Taking our time is a way of communicating that something matters to us.

As an adult apprenticing to be a metal shaper, I often retraced those same childhood mistakes, always stumbling ahead of myself. After shaping up a panel for a gas tank, I was already thinking about tacking the pieces together and welding it all up. I was anxious to reach the point where it *looked* like a gas tank. I was lured by the idea of progress, though it wasn't actual progress: It was a mirage. That's the organic nature of making things; there's no skipping ahead—it has to grow into itself.

Metal shaping, like all craftsmanship, requires an understanding of the whole, recognizing the need to follow each step to its fruition before moving on. It sounds easy—but the temptation is fierce. Enough times of having to undo my work and realizing how many hours I'd wasted eventually wised me up.

Before you become good at something, you lack the necessary forethought to take each step as it comes. You rush. After doing it a thousand times, you can better see the future. You learn to control the desire to move to the next step too quickly, because the final product demands it. That's forethought.

I WORK WITH metal for a living but wood has long been my mistress. My grandfather was a woodworker and

I can still call up the sound of his smoothing plane, the warmth of the wood, the dust on his trade books, and the smell of his shop. If my dad had a major project, we'd go out to the lumberyard and pick up a bunch of wood, tie it to the top of the car and hold it down on the way home. I spent a lot of my time in his shop in our basement, where he had a workbench: a table saw, a drill press, band saws, and cool power tools like belt sanders. Drawn to the possibility of building things, I loved going down there—sitting among the tools and material and the odds and ends, ashtrays, baseball mitts, old coffee mugs, and beer cans.

Walking into a woodshop to this day still reminds me of my childhood. The sawdust in the air, the dryness—it all takes me right back. Your sense of smell has more ties to memory than anything else, and wood always does it for me. A while back I had to move something into my truck that was buried under sawdust. When I blew the sawdust off and it took to the air, I was instantly transported back thirty years.

Wood simply never goes out of style. And it never will. It's elemental to our existence; there's something almost biological about our connection to it. Wood has been used to build structures for about ten thousand years, back to when the first wood buildings were made in England. Over the next five thousand years, the largest structure anyone built held about twenty-five people. In the following eras, the Bronze Age and Iron Age, as tools became more refined and easier to use, the homes and buildings became larger and more elaborate and complex.

From ancient Rome to Africa, the Greeks to the Chinese to the Egyptians, every civilization used wood to make functional items like tools, weapons, and shelter. Wood was the basis of construction on everything from ships to buildings to furniture like beds and stools. In the Middle Ages, wood, mostly oak, was used for all types of furniture. By the 1800s, the arrival of the Industrial Revolution allowed for mass production of new designs, as well as replications of the designs of the past.

> **When I first started doing this I thought: How can I come up with something original? People have been making chairs for centuries, millennia.**
> —ALAN KANIARZ, *furniture maker*

———————

ALAN KANIARZ MAKES wood furniture, but that doesn't come close to capturing what he does. He's a pioneer, an artist, and an innovator, carving his own path by combining old-school craftsmanship with modern technology. To Alan, the computer is just another tool. He has all his plywood CNC (computer numeral control) cut by a machine off-site into pieces in the sizes he needs to make his chairs and tables. Though the machine saves him time and money, it doesn't replace the craft. Alan still does a lot of handwork to get a finished edge on the wood and clean it all up before assembling the pieces.

Alan's work shatters the assumption that there's this distinct separation between the handmade and the technological. That wall some people put up is a myth. It's more a question of whether or not technology acts as master or partner. Craftsmanship isn't anti-technology at all. I'm actually a bit of a technology geek, fascinated by all the latest gadgets. Every craftsman works with what was once known as "technology"—I mean, a *hammer* is a technology. Even the book you are holding is a technology; it might be digitized, but it hasn't really been improved on. Maybe it can't be.

Alan is an inviting guy with a white, flowing goatee and owl-like glasses. His shop is located in an older multilevel industrial building in Detroit, part of a larger complex designed by Albert Kahn, a renowned Detroit architect. Walking into Alan's space was like entering another era: It's an old building with a collection of vintage lamps hanging from the ceiling. The shop is full of natural light, with old windows covering most of the walls. There are rooms with furniture Alan has built and restored and projects at various points in the process, waiting their turn.

Walking in there, I was like a kid in a candy store, enamored with all the tools and machines. I spotted a gigantic oscillating belt sander and something I'd never seen before: a table saw with an arm that extended outward to support large sheets of plywood. Like other modern woodworkers, Alan likes to use the Japanese pull saw, called a *nokogiri*. It's different in that it cuts as you pull it (rather than Western saws, which cut on the push motion). The movement is more natural and it's easier to follow a line, which means it takes that much longer to get tired. It's fascinating to me that the contrasting natures of our cultures are revealed through our tools: the Western idea of imposing your will on something versus the Eastern idea of working with it.

During my time with Alan I caught his contagious joy for what he does. We spent the day routing out, sanding, shaping, and gluing the wooden arc pieces for one of his signature Waldek low tables. The table's base is made up of intersecting arches of birch wood, like the threading fingers of two hands coming together. It's an adaptation of an ancient Roman design called the X chair—named for the crisscross at its base—with Alan's modern spin on it. People have been making chairs for thousands of years, so the challenge for him is figuring how to honor the tradition while also bringing in something new. Alan is stepping into a moving river and slightly altering its path. That's what craftsmen do. In a way, I think that's what everyone does in their respective disciplines—joining a tradition and leaving their mark.

Alan's designs are simple, but of course these are always the hardest to get right. The key is not adding too much, just enough to make it complete. There's an elegance and a fluidity to his pieces that make them original and eye-catching— but still purposeful. It's naked and clean and beautiful.

Alan told me he loves the moment when the forethought is cashed in, when an object is brought to life from inside his mind. "That's one of the joys of working with your hands," he said. "You take a stack of lumber and some sheets of metal, and a few hours later you have something unrecognizable from what you started with." When we were done gluing the wood pieces together, Alan finally placed the glass on top of the table. It fit, as Alan said, like it was made for it.

THERE'S AN OBVIOUS conflict between focus and forethought. Focus is about being in the moment, while fore-thought is about visualizing the future. But a craftsman needs to exist in both spaces: the single moment of the task and the future of the finished piece. It's tricky to navigate between the now and the later, but the truth is they actually feed on each other. It's balancing what's in front of you with the vision and imagination to see what doesn't yet exist.

In chess, you need to make each move carefully, but if you don't concentrate on what that move will lead to, you are going to get crushed. Some would argue that without forethought you're not even really playing chess—you're just moving pieces around. That doesn't mean you should lock yourself in—discovery and spontaneity have their role—but it means recognizing where each step is taking you.

It's almost misleading that we call what we do "work-ing with your hands." Any craftsman spends ten times as long thinking about what they're doing as engaging in the physical work. And the physical work itself is its own kind of thinking. The whole process is a conversation between the mind and the body and the object. I have to feel and listen to the material, learn how to dance with it. Lots of craftsmen talk about figuring out which way the material *wants* to go, and I know exactly what they mean. The piece has a kind of desire and a destiny all its own. This strikes me as the way we all have to interact with the world—we don't succeed by imposing our will on things with brute force; we interact with them in a back and forth manner in order to bring our aspirations to life.

**At the end of the day, you can set a piece
down on the table, it has an objective reality . . .
that's what you did today, and it lasts forever.**
—ALAN HOLLAR, *wood turner*

ALAN HOLLAR IS an imposing guy, six foot seven with a barrel chest, full white mustache, and gold hoop earring. He has a drawl that fades in and out and an affable way that softens his considerable size. We met on a freezing day in the Appalachian mountains of North Carolina, where icicles like glass sculptures hung from the gutters.

Alan is a wood turner, which means he carves pieces by spinning the wood in a lathe and holding a tool, a gouge, against it to create a shape. The principle is similar to a potter's wheel, though the lathe spins horizontally. The tool you choose, along with your hands and body posture, will directly influence the work in some obvious and not so obvious ways.

Known as the "mother of machine tools," because it gave birth to all the others, the wood lathe was likely invented by the ancient Egyptians around 1300 B.C. That first version required two people—one to do the turning with a rope, the other to do the shaping. The ancient Romans improved on the design with a turning bow, allowing one person, who knelt on the ground, to do both the spinning and the carving. It was not until the Middle Ages, with the introduction of the foot pedal, known as a treadle, that the turner was able to use both hands. The Industrial Revolution then produced machines that made the human turner no longer necessary, and the machines used today aren't too different from the ones used hundreds of years ago. Walking into a wood turner's shop today is like stepping into the historical record.

You wouldn't know it by looking at his beautiful work, but Alan Hollar is entirely self-taught. After bouncing around the country and working a wide variety of jobs as a young man, he saw a photograph of a wooden bowl in a magazine one day and was struck. *I want to do that*, he thought. So he figured out a way.

As Alan and I took a walk among the trees on his property, he compared it to living inside his own supermarket: He can't help but look at all the wood and see what it could be, what he could make out of it. He carries around this vision, this type of future sight. It's forethought on a level I hadn't even considered. I poke around shops and junkyards all the time and envision projects I can get started back home, but Alan just has to step outside to be inspired.

A wood turner begins by staring at a web of infinite possibilities. As he carves down to the finished product, he is guided by a mix of ingenuity and experience. He's navigating between what he can imagine will come about and what he *knows* will come about from doing it so many times. Like furniture maker Alan Kaniarz, Alan Hollar's favorite moment is when it comes together, when a piece reveals itself in all its glory, when it becomes what it was intended to be. After he wets the final piece with a finish, like oil, stain, or varnish, it "just goes boom . . . all the color and the figure jump right out and you can actually see—for real—what you've known in your head was going to happen."

When you make something through turning, carving, or chiseling, you obviously can't see inside, so it only reveals itself through the process, as wood is being taken away. Something that is well made gives the impression that it could not have become anything else; it has a destiny and the turner has guided it there.

After talking over coffee by the fire in his home, Alan and I threw on some work gloves and headed out into the flurrying snow to his stockpile of wood and took out a half stump that we were going to turn into a bowl. Alan had some cardboard circles to act as templates, one of which he nailed to the side of the half stump right onto the bark. We used a chain saw to remove as much extra material as was safe and then used a band saw to get down to the final size. The nail hole became our center reference, and Alan would use the hole to thread the wood onto the lathe.

Inside the shop, at the lathe, we put on goggles and got to the best part: the rhythmic whirring of the machine, the wood chips flying and covering our shirts and collecting in mounds on the floor. Alan showed me how to hold the gauge against the tool rest to cut the spinning wood by actually pinning it up against my body and then slightly turning as I cut. As we worked, the wood was spinning so fast (1,000 rpm) the sound was our only point of reference. It told us if our angle and pressure were correct. There's a music to the process, and Alan can instantly recognize a wrong note.

Because both the interior and the exterior of the bowl were to be turned, both sides of the bowl had to be mounted, or what's called "chucked." Forethought plays a huge role, because without a plan of attack you might end up with a beautiful turning but not much more. If you don't leave room for the foot of the bowl, say, you won't have anything to chuck onto in order to finish the inside. When we had gotten it down to the right size and thickness, we added a bit of design: holding a piece of wire to the bowl as we rotated it to brand a line into the wood.

Alan Kaniarz and Alan Hollar both work with wood, but their processes are mirror images of each other. Whereas Alan Kaniarz builds through addition, Alan Hollar creates through subtraction. The wood turner is figuring out what's inside. The whole thing is a "negative" process. We started with a chain saw and a log and ended with this gorgeous, delicate bowl—all by just taking things away. With Alan, I kept thinking about what Michelangelo said about his sculptures: The finished work was already there in every piece of marble. He just had to chip away at what wasn't needed. His vision and forethought were so honed that the final piece was as clear to him as if it were already in front of his eyes.

WE DON'T HAVE to be a Renaissance master to tap in to this kind of future sight, seeing what's not yet there, confident in our skills to shepherd it from idea to reality. As I grew up and moved away from building models, I took the same principles out into the world, continuing to picture what something could be. I'd look at a dilapidated car and see the jewel hidden inside of it—*We just have to flare the rear fenders, widen the track, offset the wheels, and paint it!* In my mind's eye the whole thing would be finished, but what was in front of me was a rusted piece of junk.

When I bought my first house, my girlfriend at the time was totally mystified by my excitement. It was an old and outdated place, flimsy veneer paneling on the walls. "Why are you buying this dump?" she asked me.

"What do you mean?" I said. "It's perfect for us! Can't you see it?" Then I went on and on about how all we had to do was the electrical and framing and plumbing and drywall as she stared at me like I was an alien. But I knew what I saw. We bought that house and by the afternoon of the closing, I'd already installed a dumpster in the driveway, ready to bring my vision to life.

5: SACRIFICE

I work putting my heart and soul in. I spend much more hours than I get paid for it. —JIM GASTER, *cooper*

Though sacrifice is not necessarily unique to the craftsman, it is certainly baked into the life, whether it's a whiskey distiller one false drop away from an explosion, a metal shaper an inch from crushing his hand, or anyone willing to give up basic comforts that others take for granted. I have never met a craftsman who hasn't had to make sacrifices for the work. It comes with the territory. Actually, it *is* the territory.

We need to give something up to get anything in return. That's a life principle. Most people who work with their hands for a living, who build their own business on those hands, have to be even more comfortable with sacrifice: of time, of family, of relationships, of leisure pursuits, of security, of comfort, of money.

This is never truer than when starting out.

When I was beginning as a metal shaper I was improvising as I went, walking around to shops, trying to sell my services. I said yes to jobs I couldn't do and learned how to do them as I went. A lot of craftsmen put or push themselves into situations where they're going to be forced to learn, to get in those seat hours that ultimately lead to invaluable experience. Careers are made out of the accumulation of all those yeses. To make it, you have to do your best to block out the embarrassment or insecurity that comes from stepping onto unfamiliar terrain. One of the most inhibiting obstacles toward improvement—in anything—is pride. As professionals and as people, we all suffer from it.

Building from nothing requires grabbing on to anything and everything, whether it's taking out a serious bank loan, leaning on friends or family, cashing in favors owed, or creating a long list of IOUs. It could take years of jobs that pay little more than the tools needed to complete them. You are basically working to continue working, which is far more common than people realize. There's the romance of the starving artist, but not so with the starving craftsman. But, believe me, they're out there.

Starting out, I had to be as frugal and efficient as possible. At the outset, the creature comforts are the first to go: nights at the movies, beers after work, vacations. Then you start selling off possessions, things you don't need anymore or figure you can purchase again in the future if you want to. Meals get more basic; for me, a luxury would be when I added hot dogs into the boxed mac and cheese.

When I opened my first shop, I often depended on the skylights to see what I was doing and waited until the last possible minute to turn the heat on in the winter. Before that, I worked where I lived. Many successful craftsmen—like the ones featured on *A Craftsman's Legacy*—still do that. When I meet them, I'm visiting not just their shops but also their homes. There is an unspoken intimacy because of that thin barrier. It makes their work hard to disentangle from the rest of their lives. But most craftsmen want it tangled. That's the funny thing about sacrifice—if you love what you're doing, and you're willing to give up what's needed to do it, you wouldn't even call it that. Sacrifice is what it looks like from the outside or with hindsight—but on the inside, it's passion.

> **There's no 5 percent day, 20 percent day. If I didn't put everything into what I do, that'd be letting them down.**
> —DAVID RICCARDO, *engraver*

DAVID RICCARDO GREW up in a blue-collar Western Pennsylvania town, where his dad was a boilermaker and pipe fitter. He credits that town and upbringing with his strong work ethic and deep, abiding love of working with his hands. When he was a boy, his dad took him hunting, and he was mostly fascinated by the intricate engravings on the guns. His future lay in that delicate handiwork.

Sacrifice is the ground upon which David ended up building his entire career. Married with a young child in Pennsylvania, he had a successful jewelry business when he found himself more and more drawn to hand engraving.

When he was offered an apprenticeship with a master metal engraver in Northern Michigan, he couldn't pass it up. His wife, who was also making good money in advertising, left her job, along with its health insurance and security. David sold all his jewelers' tools and everything he didn't need (along with some things he did), and his family moved hundreds of miles away to start over. They reset their life so David could pursue his craft.

After that kind of chips-down decision, David knew he had no choice but to be all in. He understood what his family had given up for him, that the sacrifice was not just his own, and he used it as a daily motivator. "They changed their lives for me to do what I want to do," he told me. Talking to David reminded me how much loved ones are part of the sacrifice story—often the part that doesn't get told.

David has a bushy beard and a big smile. He spoke casually, in a laid-back style, but it hid a fiery intensity that gradually came out over our time together. Talking to me about his work, David had that gleam in his eye, smacking one hand against the back of the other to emphasize a point. We headed across the packed snow to his shop next door, a small and comfortable building made of stone with giant exposed rocks on both the inside and outside walls. The interior surprised me, though, not quite matching the rustic surroundings: There were psychedelic pictures on the walls and skulls and rings and watches on the shelves, along with a 1960s-era raygun.*

---

* I immediately recognized the raygun as the work of sandcaster Scott Nelles, whom I knew and would later interview for an episode of the show.

So much is revealed about a person from their workspace. Their taste in decor and music, their style and inspirations and heroes, the energy around which they like to create. David's shop was extremely organized; everything seemed to have a place and reason for being there. It was a tight and intimate space, with all kinds of gravers and microscopes spread out on the table. David engraves everything from knives and guns to watches, jewelry, and even fishing rods and tattoo machines, much of it carefully set around the shop.

The engraved pieces are things of intricate beauty, with tight and crisp lines, many of which tell a story through figures and faces. You can get lost in trying to understand what they mean and why they were chosen. Working with David opened me to the idea that even if a mistake happens, you can work with it, incorporate it into the piece so it ceases to be an error. This kind of improvisation, of rolling with the punches, has led me to some of my best ideas.

First, so there's no confusion: The craftsmen are called "engravers" and the tools are called "gravers." Before gravers were mechanized, craftsmen only had palm gravers, which are long chisels or gauges with wooden palm handles. Nowadays, even when using an air-driven pneumatic drill, a person still has to use the muscle between their palm and thumb to push through the metal. A piston slaps back and forth and moves the chisel (or gauge) at a rapid speed, making a high-pitched buzzing sound, like a dentist's drill. But it takes pressure and dexterity to manipulate that gauge. From doing that repetitive motion for so many years, David has one gigantic bulging muscle that pops out of his right hand. (It's called the "thenar eminence," and David's is superhero-large.) It reminded me of the rings of a tree trunk, time and experience communicated in this case through the muscles of his body.

Our task that day was engraving a silver money clip, and because David uses a microscope to help him produce the elaborate detail in his work, I mostly couldn't see what he was doing. When it was my turn I had to get behind the lens and feel my way through it. I've been working with metal for a long time, but not like this. Engraving is incredibly exacting. It's all about technique: how you hold the machine, how much pressure you apply to it, how you manipulate the piece and your tool. You're actually moving the object you're engraving and the graver itself at the same time—in two different directions. The amount of variables at work is enough to make you dizzy.

Here's a fact that comes through on every single episode of the show: You never realize how good someone is at something until you sit down to try and do it. Peering through the microscope in David's shop, I was completely disoriented, and it was hard even to chisel a straight line. I had to learn to see the magnified piece in relation to the movement of my hand, but I could only see the metal and the tip of the tool. It takes time to train your eyes to look through the microscope; beginners often first see two broken images separated by a black spot, which is exactly what I saw.

When I finally made my first scratches, I think it was passable. David told me he could tell by the *sound* that it was okay. (That was similar to wood turner Alan Hollar, who can also sense what's working and what's not by sound.) David took the seat to fix up what I did and to engrave embellishments like scrolls on the piece. His movements were light and flowing, like how Jake Weidmann worked with his pen, the tools fluidly operating as an extension of his body. The fact that David was making scratches on metal with a dexterity reminiscent of writing with a pen shows how enormously skilled he is.

David has sacrificed years, comfort, and stability to get his craft to the level that he has reached. Like so many craftsmen, he's also a teacher, and when his students bring over their work they sometimes complain. "But it's not as good as yours," they'll say.

"I hope not!" he replies. David has had to trade in a great deal to achieve his level of quality, and he's not afraid to share that. Any teacher who doesn't communicate that struggle is doing a disservice to his students. Let them know it's hard—that's the point. It takes years of sacrifice, and they might not be willing. We tell kids they can be anything they want to be, but we should add *if you're willing to work at it*. I feel like that lesson should go hand in hand with any self-esteem we try to impart.

David Riccardo is driven by such passion for his work and his material that it's possible calling it sacrifice isn't quite right. "I'll be dead before I get to do all the things I want to do with it," David told me. That feeling, that intimate connection with what he does, is one of the reasons David calls his workshop "the church." There's birth, redemption, rebirth, communion with a larger force—it's all in there. It's where sacrifices are made and where he submits to something bigger than himself. It's a holy place.

It's hard to discuss sacrifice without touching on the idea that most people associate with professional sacrifice: money. Money is a tricky thing for me, as I think it is with a lot of craftsmen and artists. I always charge less on jobs than I should, and it's not because I'm a wonderful guy. The issue is that it's difficult to translate work hours into dollars—they're two different languages.

I don't know a whole lot of craftsmen who find it easy to figure out what to charge for a job. And it's not false humility; of course the work is worth *something*. We put our time, energy, and resources into it, it's only available that one time, and we'll never build that exact same thing again. But translating it into a number almost cheapens it. Or maybe it's beside the point. It's more like apples and oranges—a square peg in a round hole kind of problem. Obviously we need money to make a living, but a happy customer, a job well done, or the development of a friendship far outlasts the cash in my wallet.

On the show, I'm sensitive to the fact that steering the conversation with any craftsman toward money would devalue the experience. Which is not to say it's not important. The irony is you can only get really good *without* worrying about the money. It takes loving the work enough, being willing to sacrifice, to finally, hopefully make a living out of it, to get you to the point where you have something worth selling.

> **There is no life-work balance ... it's work,**
> **and you fit life in around it.**
> —APRIL WAGNER, *glassblower*

GLASS IS A ubiquitous part of our lives: drinking glasses, eyeglasses, microscope and telescope lenses, window glass that we don't always notice in everything from cars to airplanes to buildings to submarines. As my friend glassblower April Wagner told me, glass "changed the evolution of mankind in ways we aren't really conscious of and just take for granted." Before the invention of the mirror, around the fifteenth century, she said, we didn't really know what we looked like—outside of the occasional reflection in the water. Historian Ian Mortimer suggested that because of this we didn't view ourselves as individuals back then in the same way we do now. In a very literal way, glass has allowed us to know ourselves.

Mankind has been using glass since long before we figured out how to make it ourselves. Obsidian, a natural volcanic glass caused by quickly cooled lava, was originally used both for decoration and for the tips of spears in the Neolithic era, around 10,000 B.C. The earliest version of man-made glass dates back to 4000 B.C., when it was used as a glaze for stone beads in Egypt and Mesopotamia (modern-day Iraq).

The art of glassblowing was invented by the Phoenicians in modern-day Syria and Lebanon in the first century B.C. It was one of those revered skills that was passed down from apprentice to master for thousands of years by word of mouth. In fact, it was so highly secretive that many of the earliest glassblowers were forbidden to travel, lest their art spread to the rest of the world.

In the thirteenth century, the glassblowers of Venice were also kept on a secluded island, to both protect the art and to ensure that they wouldn't burn down the city. Fortunately, the glassblowers—and the craft itself—eventually seeped out and traveled all over, including to Jamestown along with the first European settlers in America.

THE FIRST TIME I met April Wagner she made it clear she was not messing around. One afternoon the phone rang at Voodoo Choppers and a woman launched into it. No hello, no greeting of any kind. "My name is April," she said. "I make glass sculptures and I need to mount them on the wall. Is that something you can make?"

"I think so," I said. "Metal, right?"

"Yeah, the guy who did it before did a shitty job, and if you're going to do a shitty job, I'm not going to hire you."

"Okay, sure. I get you."

"This stuff isn't cheap," she said, "and if it's gonna break I need to know now that you can't do this."

"Sure thing," I said. "I got it."

I made the metal shelving for her and, satisfied with my work, April contacted me again to do some other projects. I had passed her test, I guess, and we have since become friends. Now I know what a kind and gracious person she is, though she's still not afraid to be direct. I've grown to like it: In a world where so few people say what they mean, it's refreshing.

After we became friends, I invited April on one of the first episodes of *A Craftsman's Legacy*. I was fascinated by what she did and thought her life story was both inspiring and instructive. April has sacrificed a great deal for her work—and she continues to do so. As we talked, her blond hair pulled back in a ponytail, her bright blue eyes focused and intense, she admitted to not yet having mastered the work-life balance. "I *am* my work," she told me.

She's not exaggerating. Weekends, even holidays—she's working in the shop. She surrounds herself with her work, and I mean that literally as well: She lives among her inventory. I once went to drop something off at her condo, and stacks and stacks of blown-glass pieces filled every inch of the space.

Back in her early twenties, after graduating art school, April knew what she was up against. The numbers were not in her favor: Only about 10 percent of art school graduates actually make their primary living as artists. But with no savings and some hefty college loans, April pursued her dream: building her own glassblowing facility.

Beginning at the library, she did research on how to write a business plan, figured it out, and secured a bank loan that allowed her to buy a commercial space. It was an old TV repair shop, and she could only afford a few updates to it right away. She admitted to me that she made a somewhat rash decision—spending a good portion of that first loan to landscape the surrounding parking lot. She couldn't imagine being inspired to work with nothing to look at it but flat gravel and concrete. For years she lived in that commercial space, sleeping on a futon, bathing in a camping shower over an open drain, cooking her meals in a toaster oven. She traveled around to art and craft shows selling her work and, bit by bit, turned the TV repair shop into a glassblowing studio.

During every phase of construction, she'd move the futon and her tight living area to a different corner of the space, slowly progressing toward the life she wanted. She thought of it as an adventure. "When you don't have expectations," she said, "you don't have disappointment." April's early years were built on an idealism that is necessary for all artists, craftsmen, or really anyone looking to build a career out of creating something from scratch.

When we are young, we are usually more flexible about our lives, more uncompromising about our ideas, and probably also more naive about how the world works. We are more able to shut out everything else in order to pursue what we want. Most creators start out as full-throated believers in their own possibilities. We have to—I think it's the only way to get enough momentum to keep at it.

It's a self-fulfilling prophecy; only those bold enough to think they can live like this end up living like this. April told me that all the sacrifices she made didn't register that way to her at the time. Would she have done a single thing differently? Maybe she would've waited on the landscaping.

After finally getting her studio up and running, April was dealt a brutal blow. Riding her bicycle one afternoon, she was hit by a car. She was laid up in the hospital for a few weeks with a head injury, a broken rib, and a collapsed lung. Glassblowing is physically and mentally demanding work, and there was a period of time where not being able to do it again was a very real possibility. A year of physical therapy and two years of cognitive therapy were required for her to regain her lost skills. Though it was a difficult period, she came out the other end changed.

April credited that break with giving her vision and perspective, as well as time to soul search. She recognized the kind of artist she wanted to be and the kind of life she wanted to live. If she was going to make the kind of sacrifices she had to make, it should all be for work that truly moved her. So she shifted away from functional and gift items, Christmas ornaments and things "people put on the back of their toilets." April began making one-of-a-kind structural pieces.

She committed to art that spoke to *her*, that echoed what she saw in nature. "Artists are people who make things as an expression of themselves," she told me, so she started making work that aligned more with who she felt she was. The accident was a wake-up call for the life she wanted to be leading—a life surrounded by glass, its fascinating properties, and the beautiful and mysterious objects she could make out of it.

I understand the basic science behind glassblowing—and I've now done it a couple of times—but it still feels like a mystical process. The first step is the gather. April took a long and hollow stainless steel stick called a blowpipe, which is like a giant straw. She reached that into the furnace to gather the glass, which at this point is in a liquid, molten state. As she pulled it out, she continuously rotated it to keep the glass on the stick through centripetal force. She would then blow into the pipe to expand the glass. It's not a hard blow like a saxophone, as I had imagined, but just a small puff of air.

Because April was dealing with molten glass that could literally set her, her assistant, and me on fire, everything had to be meticulously done. I watched her back up carefully to sit down on a bench that had two raised rails along each side. At the bench she kept the blowpipe rotating along the rails with one hand, and with the other hand she held an oval block, which looks like giant wooden ladle, underneath the glass piece. The blocks were presoaked in water, and when the water met the glass, steam rose up; the glass actually rides that coat of steam. Every one of her movements was controlled and deliberate; her tools were all placed in a regimented manner, and every surface was extremely clean because anything can transfer to the glass or catch fire.

Then she transferred the piece onto a thinner steel rod called a punty. This exchange is extremely delicate: Her assistant came around and attached the heated punty to the other side of the glass piece (which will become its bottom) and April lightly tapped the blowpipe to separate it. As I watched April's fluid motion and concentration it kept reminding me of a dance, one that she has internalized through time and practice. All the while she was talking, explaining the process to me, and also getting up from the bench every few minutes to put the glass back into the furnace to maintain the heat. She juggled all of this amazingly well.

April understood it all so intimately: the way to use gravity, the way the glass responded to her actions, precisely what she had to do to get the glass to work with her. When the piece was done, it went into an annealing oven (or "lehr"), which comes down slowly in temperature, a process that is required because immediate cooling ("quenching") would shatter the glass. The annealing also helps remove the stress that hand-worked glass is under. It's like the recovery period patients go through after surgery; there needs to be time for the stress in their bodies to heal. As the piece cools down, it hardens, and what emerges is a gorgeous piece of handblown glass.

Glassblowing is hot, dangerous, and time-sensitive. For April, the process is a rush, a natural high. The more complicated or more invested she is, the pressure not to break it spikes her adrenaline level. She feeds off of those high stakes.

When it was my turn, I grabbed the blowpipe and immediately got a sense of the intensity. It's hard to communicate how hot the furnace really is to someone who has never done it. The glass only becomes malleable at two thousand degrees, which was blistering a few inches away. With the heat blasting at me, my forearms on fire, I had to focus on carefully gathering and bringing out the glass. It was orange and bright and I couldn't tell where the glass began or even where the edge of the furnace was. It was like trying to pick up light with my hands. At first I gathered way too much. A typical beginner mistake, April assured me. Putting in the seat time is the only way to gain that level of trust in the gather, knowing the glass is there even if you can't see it.

From the moment you take it out of the furnace, the glass is decreasing in temperature and losing its malleability, so there's a pronounced urgency to the process. When I pulled the liquid glass out of the furnace I felt the punishing heat, the blinding brightness, the fragility of the piece, the time constraint on my movements, and the gravitational pull on the glass. I had to remember to keep turning the blowpipe to prevent it from drooping. My instinct was to see gravity as a problem, but glassblowers learn to use it as a tool, an extra force they can harness, almost like a third hand. Because the glass is molten and can't be touched, the glass artist can use gravity to shift it around on either of the sticks.

On top of all of these moving parts, glassblowers only have one shot to get it right or they have to start all over. A metal engraver, for example, can go as slow as he needs, and I remember David Riccardo hovering behind me while I was engraving, saying, "No hurry, no hurry," like a mantra. But glass is a whole different beast.

"Glass is really about the things you can't see: centripetal force and gravity and temperature and timing," April told me. Even facing all these elements, she never *seems* hurried. I think of David MacDonald, who sat next to me at his potter's wheel, throwing at the same speed as I was, but I could tell he was seeing it all in slow motion. He had it all under control, whereas it was as if my hair was on fire. April reminded me of one of those superheroes who operate at super speed; in order for the regular person to see what Wonder Woman sees, the bullets are presented in slow motion.

And when it's all done, April has created gorgeous, eye-popping pieces of color and light. They're breathtaking. "I find pride and value in the response I get from my work by other people," April told me, and that doesn't necessarily mean someone who buys a piece from her; it applies to anyone who comes in contact with her work and has an emotional response to it. They may not know what goes into it, but the final piece is the result of hard work and sacrifice, like pressurized coal revealing a diamond.

6: FALLING FOR BIKES

As far back as I can remember, I have been fascinated by three things: motorcycles, helicopters, and scuba diving. They seemed like the apex of what a person could do on land, air, and sea. (To this day, one of my fantasies is to jump off a helicopter into the water, like a Coast Guard Rescue Swimmer.) I still have memories of being a five-year-old at the local city fair and seeing the police department's display of their cars, bikes, and a helicopter with a giant bubble in front like I'd seen on *M*A*S*H*. In my room I hung a photograph of me on their 1970s Harley Davidson police motorcycle, a big black-and-white FLH model with saddle-bags and lights. That picture had so many pinholes from moving around over the years.

I didn't know at the time that they would come to define my life, but something about motorcycles spoke out to me. They were messages beamed from a different planet and a force luring me in. To my young eyes and ears they were in bright color and at full volume while everything else was a muttering gray. I was into choppers, which are motorcycles where the neck is lifted higher and the front end is made longer. To move the neck you have to have cut it first, "chop" it. The chopper looks like a stretched-out version of a standard bike. They're about attitude: big, unruly, and built to get attention.

The first chopper I remember seeing was a Triumph in my friend's driveway when I was a kid. It was run-down and sun-faded with a dull old black paint job. It showed up like a comet in my world. I never heard it run or saw it roll, and the next time I went over to my friend's the bike was gone, remaining this frozen version of cool for years afterward. From that point on, I wanted more. After school or on weekends I would ride my bicycle out to the Honda dealership to check out all the motorcycles, fantasize about which one I'd get, and imagine hopping on one and just riding off.

When I was eight, my uncle got a yellow Suzuki RM80, a dirt bike, which he said I could ride it if I could start it. This was actually a trick: not he, my grandfather, or my dad ever thought I would be able to. Every time I went over to my uncle's house I'd drag it out of the garage and kick it and kick it, often for over an hour, trying to get it going. Every once in a while I would manage a little sputter, which was enough of a tease to keep me at it. Exhausted and dejected, I'd eventually give in and roll it back into the garage. But sure enough, the next time we went over there I'd run over to try again.

A few months into this routine, I kicked it one afternoon and the engine miraculously started rapping away. I was astounded. "It started!" I yelled, to no one in particular. "It started!" I hopped on. In preparation for this glorious moment, I already knew the bike's shift pattern, though I didn't exactly know *how* to shift, or use a clutch. Once the bike was running, I didn't wait for someone to stop me, and I drove up and down the street in first gear. I think my family was more surprised than I was; stunned, really. Though I wasn't traveling that fast, the engine was winded up loud because I couldn't get out of first gear. That didn't matter to me; it was the first time I got in the wind, and I knew I'd found my thing.

I was twenty years old when I bought a bike of my own, a Yamaha 650, a street bike, which I got off a guy at work. It was dirty and cheap, full of a lot of extras, like a windscreen and bags. A few months later the same guy sold me his old Harley Sportster, which had a long front end, a sissy bar on the back, and buckhorn handlebars. That bike was a mess, and I spent countless hours kicking it trying to get it to start. Once it finally did, it would dance all over the place on its kickstand. About two weeks in I decided to take it all the way down and completely rebuild the bike. Some shops helped me out and some ripped me off, seeing me a mile away for the green kid I was. (I'd hold on to those memories years later when customers brought their bikes to me, never wanting anyone to feel taken advantage of.)

But I loved that bike—probably *because* of all the work it needed. It gave me the chance to tinker and build and create and play. A new bike would've been easier to ride, but it wouldn't have taught me as much. That beat-down Harley forced me to take the time to learn it inside and out, get a sense of its bones and blood. I still like to embrace the friction and pushback I get from things that don't come easily. That process of clashing against the world, having to find my way, is how I end up with something new.

Motorcycle riding offers this connection as well: the link between you and the bike and the one between the bike and the world. You feel every little groove, pebble, and curve in the road, the wind on your face and body, the world pushing back against you and you against it. You're taking in all the elements: the rhythmic pattern of the motor, the whirring of the tires on the cement, the mechanical sound of the chain running in the sprocket like a firm handshake. The old Shovelhead Harley sounds so noisy and mechanical that you'd think it had serious problems if you didn't know better. But that's just the sound of it working, producing horsepower by shooting off that raw sound and feeling.

A motorcycle preserves that lost connection to the world outside. In the classic book *Zen and the Art of Motorcycle Maintenance*, Robert Pirsig wrote about how through a car's windshield, everything is just more television. But "on a cycle you're *in* the scene, not just watching it." When riding, I'm no longer a spectator. I am inside of it; I *am* the show. The world and I are one.

A car ride today is like being in a spaceship: media screens, satellite radio menus, GPS, and a climate-controlled environment. The interior is a cocoon, hermetically sealed in a way that pushes the engine—and all of the car's mechanics—into the distance. All we hear is a hum, if anything at all. The modern driver gets a sense of this plastic isolation upon rolling down a single window—especially a back window. The car is so aerodynamic that the flow of air is broken, creating a reverberation, which shakes the car with a booming drone. It's like a blunt reminder that you and the outside world are separated. (Cracking another window will balance it out.)

Modern cars are designed to protect you from the physical experience of the road. You're supposed to forget what you're doing—whether it's the things the car can do without you, the quiet of the engine, or the smoothness of the ride. In fact, the best cars are considered the ones that shut out the universe completely. A motorcycle does the opposite: It opens you up to the world.

WHEN I WAS thirteen, my dad lost our nursery and fertilizer business and I started working for a lawn company. Weekends, summers, vacations, I'd be on my bicycle at seven a.m. heading to work. Then I'd hop in the bed of the pickup truck with guys a decade older than me and we'd cut lawns. I was a quiet kid who kept mostly to myself anyway; with no headphones or any other distraction, the work gave me time to imagine and dream.

In high school, I started working at Xerox as a stock boy. My parents had always talked about college, but I couldn't find the motivation to apply myself in school. I wanted to start making money and buying things for myself. After graduation, Xerox offered me a full-time job with benefits, including paid vacation, so I took it. There was room for advancement and I didn't have many other choices.

My plan was to one day go into accounting to work along-side my dad, who by that point had gone into finance management. I did some community college on and off, but it didn't take more than an episode of my favorite TV show for me to skip class. Through my twenties I worked my way up at Xerox, trying to find my niche. Once I stumbled into IT, I found it. It was an area I was good at and enjoyed: making and building things. I was a computer nerd who was fascinated by technology, and I visited computer stores the same way that I visited the Honda motorcycle dealership—with big eyes and bigger dreams.

Since this was the start of the digital era, I was in the right place at the right time, and I threw myself into it. Way over my head and anxious to learn, I pored through networking and computer books on my own time, soaking up as much as I could as fast as I could. Every step of the way, I did what I could to learn more, to move ahead, to broaden my responsibilities. I'm sure that came from how I grew up, taking on any project that needed to be done around the house and working with my dad. That ethic would become instrumental a few years later when I set out on my own without much of a map or idea what I was doing.

After a few years with Xerox, I moved into management, part of the natural progression of working at a company. But the spark had gone out. I had a better salary and title, but without the creativity, freedom, and challenge of my old job. Through those years I always escaped by working on my bike in my garage. I bought parts at a retail place nearby, which was also a makeshift shop that did repairs on the side. They didn't have any table lifts for the bikes, but a few mechanics would pitch in and work in the showroom on the floor. Eventually I offered to help out.

The woman who owned and ran the shop was kind and boisterous, in her midthirties, skinny with hair down to her waist. She was also confident, having grown up around motorcycles, and generous, happy to teach what she knew. In the evenings, I spent my free time working as a mechanic at her place in exchange for free parts for my own bike: I'd change a head gasket on one of their bikes and get an ignition system for my own.

Wrenching on bikes wasn't something I thought about pursuing, like moving up at Xerox or taking classes or working with my dad. I didn't know anything about how a shop ran, couldn't conceive of what it would take. The idea of actually doing it for a living wasn't even on my radar.

7: RESPECT

Before enlightenment, chop wood, carry water.
After enlightenment, chop wood, carry water. —ZEN SAYING

Voodoo Choppers has evolved over time, but not in the way people normally use that term in business, meaning a growth in size. It has gone through the opposite process, a simplification, a necessary streamlining. A few years back, I had a handful of employees, a backlog of work, and a two-year waiting list. Having built the business from nothing, I was proud of what Voodoo had become, but something was wrong. I had been traveling so much for appearances at bike rallies that I was losing contact with what I loved in the first place: the work. I was building my brand, but that's not why I had gotten into this.

When I stopped traveling, I apologized to my employees but let just about all of them go. I explained that I wanted to get back to working with my hands again, and that's what

I did. The business's output slowed down considerably, and it was a difficult time. But I got back in touch with what I loved about bike building, and I also felt that I was reconnecting with my customers. In the end, I gave myself over to a simple maxim: *Respect the customers, respect the work.*

A finished bike is a cumulative result of how well each individual part has been completed and how much care has been put into it. Those are the bones of the work. At the base of all of that is a foundation of respect. A craftsman comes off as a type of illusionist. All their skill and knowledge is practically invisible; they move swiftly and effortlessly and efficiently and purposefully. They're hiding all that time they spend trying and thinking and failing and questioning and stumbling. The outside observer can't see it, but it's all in there.

> **I feel like we have this gap in the last hundred years where we've replaced a lot of things and made it more uncomfortable than it needs to be.**
> —SETH GOULD, *blacksmith*

SETH GOULD IS a blacksmith, a toolmaker, a teacher, and a fellow lover of hammers. A viewer of *A Craftsman's Legacy* contacted me to tell me about Seth, and after I learned about him and his work, he became a hero of mine. He is a metalsmithing rock star, and I was excited to meet and work with him.

I traveled out to Penland School of Crafts, a craftsmen mecca in the Blue Ridge Mountains of North Carolina. To get there I had to drive up into the mountains and navigate tight roads carving through the stunning hills. Then in the vastness, the campus unfolded before me. It was like a hidden community in the mountains—newer buildings of white stone mixed with various work sheds made of wood. It's a picturesque, magical place where the light bounces off the windows just right and the sky goes on forever.

Seth moved out to Penland with his wife to live, teach, and work as a resident artist, an intensive three-year commitment. One of the most prestigious craftsman programs in the country, Penland is like an incubator, a rare opportunity for people to explore their craft and not have to worry too much about outside distractions. It's an intense yet nurturing environment for craftsmen to fully develop their potential and help advance their discipline. I didn't even know places like this existed; I wish I had.

Seth is a relaxed guy, around thirty, with a shaved head, earrings, and a ubiquitous smirk. A native New Englander, he has a likable mix of quiet humility and total assuredness about who he is and what he does. His relationship with tools goes way back, though like with so many craftsmen, there were some detours along the way. Seth first fell in love with tools while growing up around his father and grandfather's automotive shops. Though he had no idea what most of the tools did, he was drawn to the look, the feel, the weight, and the sounds they made striking something else.

In college, Seth was an art student, on track for a degree in graphic design. But when he found himself in a metalsmithing class, it opened up this whole new path. He took to the craft in a way that felt almost preordained, reconnecting with that young curious kid in his dad's shop. Working with his hands and with metal led him into jewelry work and then conceptual art pieces. But it was making his first hammer that told Seth he'd found his destiny. Holding it in his hand and realizing "the tool worked and that's all it did" just struck him. It was simple and elegant enough that it needed no explanation. It identified itself.

By good fortune, Seth got a chance to learn from one of the premier blacksmiths of Colonial ironwork, Peter Ross, a craftsman whose work is rooted in a different century. Ross forges metal himself and approaches his work from a historically accurate perspective; he cares as much about how his tools are made as how they look. What Seth gained from his mentor was a respect for the process, the traditions and techniques that have lasted for centuries, and how they laid the groundwork for everything else.

While Seth has a foot in the past, his other one is firmly planted in the present. He's not interested in simply paying homage. He wants to honor his forebears—"preserve the essence," in his words—while also moving the craft of metalsmithing forward. At Penland these days, Seth is working on what I would call "lockboxes." The historical term is "coffer," but Seth bristles at using it, because it implies a replication of an old object; he aims to put a contemporary spin on them. Seth is an interesting case because his work exists at this intersection of craft and art. When I asked if he considers himself a craftsman or an artist, he said both terms flow back and forth in his mind, but in the end, he's happy to leave the classification to others.

THE BLACKSMITH IS often called the King of All Trades because he can make his own tools. This fact put the toolmaker in a priority place in society from the beginning. Tools were so central to previous eras that the names of epochs came from the materials used to make them: the Stone age, the Bronze age, and the Iron age. Some episodes of the show are far outside of my wheelhouse, but others feel like my natural habitat. For twenty years I've worked with all kinds of metal, and I've swung hammers just about every day of my adult life.

Seth told me "there's something about being surrounded by things you made," and his shop is filled with his own hammers, calipers, saws, and other tools. Being with another hammer lover sent me down the rabbit hole. We talked about how each one has a different shape, size, angle function, feel in your hand—almost a distinct personality.

When I visited Seth, we made a cross peen hammer, popular with blacksmiths. It has a narrow, horizontal striking surface, helpful for when the full face of the hammer is too large or when you're trying to reach a specific area. To get started, he took a hockey puck–sized piece of steel and threw it in the forge, knowing based on time and color when it was hot enough and malleable enough to take out.

Then we used a power hammer to resize the piece into a typical rectangular head. A power hammer is a large machine in which you step on a foot pedal to bring the top part, the ram, smashing down on the anvil, which sits on the bottom part. (It can do amazing things to an empty beer can.) A skilled craftsman like Seth can achieve great control over this beast of a machine, and he has to work quickly, because like glass, hot metal comes with a time constraint. There's a specific cadence to each machine, and a craftsman will sync up with its rhythm, knowing precisely how long it takes for the shaft to cycle fully and how quickly it drops. Those unique features get internalized by his body; it's like the way a hockey player knows the specific feel and character of *his* stick, no matter how similar it may look to other ones.

In Seth's shop, I got into the flow of the work, and my confidence skidded into cockiness. When we were punching out the eye of the hammer to fit in the wood handle, Seth asked me to do the honors. He was holding the metal piece in place for me to strike down on it, but instead of choking up on the six-pound sledgehammer, I swung it like Thor. I missed hitting the metal square on, and it flew out of Seth's hand and ricocheted around the floor. I felt like a complete jackass and the cameras cut. "It's okay," Seth said, in his genial deadpan. "That happens."

It was embarrassing; I've been working with metal too long to make mistakes like that. That sequence isn't in the episode, but I almost wish it were. It shows that the reality isn't always so clean, especially if the worker is sloppy. I had let my respect for the tools and the process slip and it came back to bite me. Fortunately no one got hurt. When sparks are flying and you're inches away from something that literally could crush your hand and you're manipulating a piece of steel that's over two thousand degrees, you better remember to respect your equipment and materials, because you'll lose a finger if you don't.

But mistakes are still inevitable. I've had gasoline shoot from a pressurized nozzle into my eyes, and I've had metal bounce off my face and lodge in my eyeball. That time I had to have the metal drilled out so it wouldn't rust in there. (This actually just happened again the other day, while I've been working on this chapter.) I've had all kinds of cuts, lacerations, and burns. Each one is a little reminder to me: *Pay attention, idiot.* In the first magazine spread I ever did, my forearm is wrapped in bandages and gauze, because I had burned it badly on a fender. It's the price you pay for working with something that powerful. You're never too far from some kind of catastrophe.

Seth traveled to Japan at an impressionable time in his career and marveled at the material and ornamentation work there, with styles that "caught my eye and blew my mind," he told me. We talked about the differences between East and West, and how they can be seen not just in style but in attitude and approach, something that has always intrigued me. The same skills developed along different tracks, influenced by the cultures, values, and habits of a people. Though much of the respect for craftsmen has faded away in America, there is a clear lineage in the East, a continuity and appreciation of craftsmen throughout the centuries.

We talked about our desire to see this country re-embrace craftsmanship, but Seth then became reluctant; he said he felt that if he can keep his trade going and he can make a living, that's enough. Though his humility prevented him from saying it, or even seeing it, I believe he's having a huge impact. The tools Seth makes—hammers, dividers, calipers, saws, scales—are used every day by craftsmen. And every time people see his work in either a museum or a store, or have an opportunity to talk to him about it, they are developing an appreciation for craftsmanship. Even if they don't buy anything or ever see it again, they walk away with a little more respect for the craft, for the process, for the history, and for the person behind it.

> **I'm not out there doing this all on my own. I'm doing this all on the shoulders of the previous generations that developed the knowledge and the technique and the tools, and I'm just carrying that forward.**
> —WALTER ARNOLD, *stone carver*

KNOCKING A SHARP edge into stone to create a design, weapon, or tool might just be in man's DNA. Stone carving dates back to 10,000 B.C., and some version of it showed up in practically every ancient civilization. In fact, stone carvings are considered to be the very first evidence of civilization that archeologists have found. When our ancestors, around 3000 B.C., discovered iron, it represented a great leap forward, because they had at last found a material stronger than the stone we were cutting into, one that could be carved more exactly and withstand rigorous use.

Among the most historic stone carvings ever made is the Great Sphinx of Giza, built in Egypt around 2500 B.C. To this day it remains one of the great accomplishments on Earth. A half man, half lion carved into Giza plateau's limestone, the Sphinx is both a marvel and a mystery: How it was made without any machinery whatsoever and what exactly its purpose was are still topics of fierce debate among experts.

The stone carvers' tools continued to be refined through the discovery and improvement of various metals and processes over the years. When guilds became popular in the Middle Ages, carvers joined together to help ensure their livelihoods. They agreed on formal training, quality standards, and an economic system that included fair competition.

MY FIRST REALLY difficult interview experience for *A Craftsman's Legacy* was with Walter Arnold, a stone carver out of Chicago whom we featured in season one. Walter is a quiet and humble man who works by himself a lot and is not a naturally gregarious person. He was guarded during the first part of the interview inside his house, and I wasn't yet skilled enough to draw him out. When it felt like our conversation wasn't quite getting rolling, our director pulled me aside. "Hey, Eric," he said, "let's go into the shop and start working. Get him to talk in there."

So we set up in Walter's shop, a gigantic place attached to his house, with high square windows, sculptures laid out, stone piled up, and a calcified, white dust covering every surface. Air lines (thin hoses that powered his chisels) dangled from the ceiling. Almost immediately Walter became more animated, cracking jokes and telling stories. We began speaking like just two guys having a conversation, which is exactly the idea.

What's intriguing about the stone carver's craft is that, though air-driven chisels came about in the nineteenth century, the tools and technique remain not much different than they were thousands of years ago. Although Walter sometimes uses air tools, he also regularly employs a hammer and chisel exactly the way his forebears would. The through-line from the very first stone carvers to today's is a particularly straight and well-defined line—and Walter's story illustrates this well.

Walter was an unusual child, to the say the least. By the age of twelve he knew what he wanted to do with his life—and it was not something with any currency in the 1960s Midwestern world he was born into. He ignored pretty much everyone who told him stone carving was a dead craft, impossible to learn; he had an almost obsessive desire to figure out how to do it. Drawn by its beauty and its history, he set out to teach himself as much as he could.

The desire was partly planted at a young age by his parents, who exposed Walter to a steady stream of the arts: symphonies, museums, and travel. As a child, he spent his Saturdays taking classes at the famed Art Institute of Chicago, which brought in artists and craftsmen for demonstrations.

The Arnolds lived near the University of Chicago's magnificent campus, built in the collegiate gothic style, an offshoot of the nineteenth-century gothic revival. The medieval-inspired limestone buildings with gargoyles and other carvings provided endless wonder for Walter. When school let out he'd hop on his bike and ride around the campus in awe at the structures and figures, wondering how he could create something like that.

Walter grew up during an era of urban renewal in the city, a time when brick and stone buildings were being torn down. He would go through his neighborhood dragging his red wagon, grab chunks of limestone from these sites, and drag them back home to mess around with in his dad's basement workshop. As the old city was being thrown away, its pieces were being used by a young boy to carve his future.

Walter didn't know what he was doing down there in his dad's shop, poking around on the stone first with hammers and screwdrivers and then with art store chisels. But he plugged away through his teenage years, asking friends to sit for him as he figured out how to make busts of their heads. It's impressive what he was able to accomplish on his own, but at some point he realized he was "trying to reinvent the wheel." He needed to go where the action was.

When Walter was sixteen, a searching teenager in ripped blue jeans, he hitchhiked out to Washington, D.C., to the National Cathedral, a neogothic stunner of a building on which construction began in 1907. (It would become the nation's second biggest cathedral when it was finally completed in 1990.) His goal was to be taken under the wing of one of the older Italian carvers working onsite. They were friendly enough, allowing him to ask questions and see their shops before sending him on his way. But Walter was not deterred. He went home, enrolled at the University of Illinois, and devoured as many art history classes as he could. He figured the old masters from centuries ago could teach him more than just about anyone.

A few years later, as an idealistic young man of twenty, Walter decided to literally go to the source—to the Tuscany region of Italy, near Carrara, where the world's most prized marble is quarried. Where the masters still live and work. Where a straight line can still be drawn back to the Renaissance. "I figured if anything's going on it's happening there," he told me. It's like the headwaters of the entire craft. Marble has been "the lifeblood" of the area since Roman times, and the location is still the largest producer of marble in the world. The name Carrara is synonymous with the world's finest marble.

Many of the stories craftsmen tell me are about searching for some earlier incarnation of their trade, like the way Seth Gould trained under Peter Ross. But Walter was so committed that he literally went to where it all began. In Italy, he talked his way into a shop with two older carvers, who between them had 110 years of experience. In his time there, Walter absorbed everything he could from them as well as the other carvers who would come through the shop.

Walter happened to be in a fortuitous position. The children and grandchildren of these carvers hadn't taken to the craft, and the carvers didn't want them to. They wanted their kids to be bankers and car salesmen, to clock regular hours and wear clean suits and ties. When Walter showed up, an American kid with an all-consuming desire to learn, these older carvers saw a way to pass their craft on—without having to worry about arming the competition. Walter struck gold; he had walked into a tradition that was in danger of dying out and became a repository for the knowledge that needed somewhere to flow.

Three years later, back in America, Walter was finally able to get a job working on the National Cathedral. For five years he carved animals, stone columns, and gargoyles alongside fifth-generation carvers who had honed their skills on the cathedrals of Europe. In 1985, his tenure there ended and he returned to Chicago and opened his own studio.

Some of Walter's tools are historical artifacts, including a chisel from the late 1880s. Like most tools that last that long, it has a story of its own. It was given to him by a mentor who had worked on the iconic Gothic revival *Chicago Tribune* building in the 1920s. Walter himself later did restoration work on that very same tower, using that very same chisel—another example of the cycle that characterizes the world of craftsmen.

On a shelf high up in Walter's shop was a row of heads in plaster casts and limestone, the ones Walter had made of his teenage friends. Next to the busts was a large limestone carving he did of his own hand—the craftsman's instrument. I also spotted a carving of a creature made of a beautiful, bright white marble that looked almost like soap. Walter had gotten the material while in Italy, from the same mountain in Tuscany where in the 1500s Michelangelo got his marble, which the Renaissance master described as "reminiscent of sugar."

Walter's pieces are mostly classical, and he described them as "very structured, like working from a score"—but he maintains an undying love for gargoyles, demonic and strange and alluring. Gargoyles originated in ancient Egypt but began to spread in medieval Europe. They were used decoratively, religiously, and functionally on the exteriors of churches. The religious aspect was to scare parishioners into believing that evil lurked outside the church. The functional aspect was to direct water away from the stone building. Walter is attracted to the way that carving gargoyles is "improvisational, like jazz"; he's freer to invent and change course in the midst of working on a piece.

Walter's carvings are a bit eerie: The bared teeth and eyes are so lifelike, especially when the light hits them just right. Walter explained that carving depends less on shape and form and much more on light and shadow. The artist uses those things to create depth and the illusion of movement while also animating the features of a face. It reminded me of the way glassblowers like April Wagner use gravity—a natural force that the craftsman learns how to work with instead of against. Time and time again, craftsmen reiterate this principle: working with what's available and seeing even the obstacles as tools. I feel it's a universal lesson.

Walter's episode was also the first time (though not the last) that the craft itself was genuinely difficult for me. He works with a pneumatic chisel, which is air-driven, because it's faster and easier on his body. Using that correctly requires proper technique: the angling, the amount of power, the pressure, the way to approach the piece, being able to see the work and then remove what's not necessary. After I struggled to carve a leaf into limestone, Walter picked up his pneumatic chisel and knocked out the shape as automatically as if he were signing his name.

Respect touches each and every part of this craft. There's respect for the centuries-old techniques. There's respect for the tools, which can easily break from the friction with the stone, as well as respect for the stone itself, which is a gift from the Earth and, in the case of Michelangelo's marble, an opportunity to touch history. There's respect for the people and craftsmen of the past, to whom Walter owes his livelihood. And then there's respect for the future generations, who will inherit all of it because people like Walter deemed it worthy enough to keep the traditions alive.

Walter embodies the idea that a craftsman is partly a vessel for the craft—shepherding it along across time and space. In his shop, he spoke eloquently about that connection, the way it places him along a continuum of craftsmen and how he occupies one space in that line.

And that story continues. When Walter was in Italy, the master carvers directed him to the sculptures in a particular cemetery in Genoa, pieces their grandfathers and uncles had worked on. He went up to the cemetery—the Camposanto di Staglieno—and it nearly blew his mind. The sculptures were unlike anything he had ever seen, massive pieces, fifteen feet high, elaborately detailed and meticulously carved, far past what he had thought was possible. The cemetery happens to include the largest outdoor sculpture museum in Europe and the most astounding collection of nineteenth-century to mid-twentieth-century Italian marble sculpture.

Almost forty years later, Walter regularly returns to that cemetery for inspiration. He wrote a book about it, and in recent years he has been leading an international effort to restore the hundreds of sculptures there, many of which have fallen into disrepair. It's the most fitting way he could think to repay those who taught him the trade. The restoration will ensure that those pieces exist for future generations, so that some young child might be inspired by seeing them as they were meant to be seen. Just like how, as a boy, Walter himself was once transported on his bicycle at the University of Chicago or as a hitchhiking kid outside the National Cathedral.

"The more they understand this," he told me, "the more they see what's around them. You live in a city with carvings done a hundred years ago and never look at it, but once you understand what it is you start seeing it and enjoying it." And that's true wherever you live: A walk around any downtown will likely reveal the handiwork of generations of carvers. Walter told me we can give them their due by remembering to look up from time to time, instead of rushing to another meeting or staring at our phones. Since talking with Walter I find myself constantly looking up, especially in old towns and cities, unwilling to let all the beauty and history pass me by. It's my way of tipping my hat, showing respect, to the generations of craftsmen who came before me.

8: THE GIVE-AND-TAKE

To see anything in relation to other things is to see it simplified. —EDITH HAMILTON, *author and educator*

No matter what it is we do—as a profession, a hobby, or even a lark—we're all making our way through the larger cycle. We occupy a place somewhere in that progression and can gain something from anyone, anywhere on that same cycle. I've always seen craftsmen as the spokes of the wheel—with the past, present, and future all spinning around us.

Frank Shamrock, a mixed martial arts (MMA) fighter, champion, and educator, has developed a system called plus, minus, equals: All his fighters need someone to learn from, someone to teach, and someone at their level to compete with. It's a way to maintain continuous and valuable feedback about where you are in your craft, giving you the bigger picture. "False ideas about yourself destroy you," Shamrock has said. "For me, I always stay a student . . . you have to use the humility as a tool."

When I read about Shamrock's system, I immediately responded to it. I carry a similar approach to my own craft and my life. We're all beginners, amateurs, professionals, and teachers at *something*. Some of these phases aren't as cut-and-dried as they sound. For instance, even if you've only been at it a short time, you have something to share, like a fresh set of eyes, which is enormously valuable. And even if you've been doing it your whole adult life, you have still something to learn from that new perspective.

True artists and craftsmen want to both share and expand their knowledge. The skills they've acquired are often thousands of years old, and they recognize their responsibility to not only keep the craft alive but to contribute to its future. In earlier eras, students attended a university to study and explore and *add something* to their discipline, whether that was medicine or astronomy or philosophy. Though of course some college students nowadays approach their education this way, it no longer seems to be the primary goal.

Apprenticeships, one alternative to traditional education, have become more rare in modern times. There's an integrity to the apprenticeship process that's worth preserving: Because of the way the process works, the student is encouraged to become a teacher in the future, ensuring the skill lives on.

There's an emotional aspect at work as well. Research has shown time and again that depression can be cured through giving back, that we are happier and more content when we are giving than when we are taking. I think that's because it offers us agency in the world and it makes us feel less alone. We all crave human connection, and finding a way to give openly and unselfishly provides us with that.

One thing I used to enjoy doing was grabbing my portable English wheel and some scraps of aluminum and setting up at bike rallies. An English wheel is the primary machine a craftsman uses to shape metal—it has only been slightly improved on since its invention during medieval times. The machine looks like a C-clamp, with a top wheel and lower wheel (the anvil), and you place a thin piece of metal in between. The adjustment screw sets the distance between the two wheels, and then you repeatedly push the metal in and out to shape it. It's relatively basic in principle but difficult to execute properly (which the simplest things often are). I'd set up for a couple of hours at rallies to show anyone who was curious about shaping metal.

People would gather around and ask questions, and I'd explain how it worked and then let them try it. It was an opportunity to teach something I love, to meet other bike enthusiasts, and to share my craft. They also get the chance to see the process of making a motorcycle and to see how much work goes into it. Maybe at the end of the day they could appreciate why a custom fuel tank costs a few thousand dollars.

Sometimes, other shapers would hear about me giving these demonstrations and give me a hard time. "You can't do that," they'd say. "Why are you giving away secrets like that for free?"

It was surprising, and my response was likely defensive. "What's so secretive about it?" I'd shoot back. I didn't invent metal shaping; it's hundreds of years old and it's not mine to guard. Knowledge isn't a zero-sum game where you lose it by giving it away. It actually *multiplies* by my sharing. The craft expands.

I feel it's a privilege to show what I do. If I light a candle for someone, if that has them wanting to learn more—take a class, work as an apprentice, even just watch a YouTube video—then I'm doing my job. That's the point, in my opinion. I'm not interested in going to the grave with any of this.

> **A hundred and fifty years after I'm done,
> they'll forget who I am probably. Wilson Capron
> will just be a dude of the past. But I would love for
> someone to look at a bit or pair of spurs I've done and
> say, "I have no idea who that is but that's incredible."**
> —WILSON CAPRON, *bit and spur maker*

WILSON CAPRON IS a Texas guy down to his bones. He's a genial soul, generous with his workspace and open about his story, which is an inspiring one. From a young age, Wilson was immersed in cowboy culture: His dad was a ranch manager in West Texas, and his family was responsible for 150,000 acres of farmland and some one thousand cows.

Wilson's dream was to be a rodeo cowboy. Rodeos emerged out of the competitions of ranch hands back in the 1880s. In his twenties, his sport was team roping, which requires two people: a "header," who gets out in front of the steer and tries to rope its horns or head, and a "heeler," who gets behind it and has to then rope its hind legs. The timing and cooperation between the two ropers—and their horses—takes dedicated hours of practice. In order to finance his rodeo dreams, along with the entry fees to competitions, Wilson found a job helping out a friend who ran a bit and spur manufacturing plant. At the time, it was a means to an end, a pit stop on his way to rodeo glory. But the job would end up changing his life.

Bits and spurs are part of the tools of communication between a rider and a horse. A bit is the piece of metal that goes into the horse's mouth and is connected to the reins, and together they comprise the bridle. The purpose is to allow the rider to guide and send commands—through his hands—to the horse. Spurs are attached to the back of the cowboy boots. They can be decorative but they serve a purpose; the rider uses them to apply pressure, telling the horse when and how to move. As long as they're used the right way, by someone with experience and proper leg control, spurs do not hurt the animal.

Wilson was open to learning the craft of bit and spur making, but it wasn't until he learned how to engrave, and saw the intricate artistry involved, that he knew his rodeo days were over. He had found his true love. Wilson's dad was also a painter, and that desire to create was likely in his son's blood from the beginning. He just hadn't found his outlet yet.

It's striking how often I've heard a version of Wilson's story: Somebody spends time and energy chasing what he thinks is his dream. Then he ends up getting sidetracked, which turns out not to be a sidetrack at all. Call it fate. Call it destiny. Maybe the original thing was only a pathway to his true calling the whole time. I believe there is a purpose to our lives and we're always either choosing or rejecting the steps that lead us to it.

At the time Wilson abandoned his rodeo career for bits and spurs, high-end spurs weren't popular enough for him to make a living. Having fallen in love with engraving, he thought about switching over to guns or knives, which are popular choices for engravers—there's always a market for those. But he couldn't walk away.

He was captivated—these were the tools of the real cowboy, intimately tied to his Texas roots. Wilson understood what authentic cowboys were all about, and he was always irked by the Hollywood stereotype of the uneducated drunk looking for a fight. He wanted to keep the real cowboy tradition alive, and his craft took on the contours of a mission: If people didn't work to preserve and spread the tradition of what cowboys actually were, then the fiction would be all that was left. Fortunately, the market for bits and spurs happened to catch up right as Wilson was hitting his stride, and he made engraving them his livelihood.

Bridle bits, and especially spurs, narrow the gap between art and craftsmanship. There's a beauty to the spur and its interlocking parts, and an aspect of that beauty comes from their utility: The cowboy actually *needs* them. During my visit to his shop in Central Texas, I mentioned to Wilson that one of his sets of engraved spurs seemed too beautiful to wear, and his eyes popped. That's exactly what he was going for, he told me. He wanted people to be torn, to say, "I have to put it on, I have to use it, but it's so pretty I can't."

Spurs go back to the time of Julius Caesar, when Roman fighters needed a way to keep their hands free to fight while still being able to steer their horses. The distinctive spiked disk at the end of the spur, which makes the noise—the thing that people think of as the whole spur—is actually called a "rowel." The entire spur encompasses the U-shaped device that wraps around the heel of the boot.

The rowel spur that we would recognize today originated in England and France around the fourteenth century. In medieval times, during the days of knights, a person's spurs were a mark of their rank—gold, silver, tin. It was the way to know where someone stood in the pecking order. (It's where we get the still-used phrase *Earn your spurs*.) Over the centuries, various styles of spurs grew wherever a cowboy culture developed. Wilson's engraving style is a mix from California, Mexico, and Texas, each of which has its own characteristics and designs.

Derived from the Spanish *vaquero*—from *vaca* for "cow"—
the word "cowboy" originally referred to animal herders in
Mexico who rode on horseback, though American culture
created its own distinct version. The number of cowboys in
the American West peaked during the age of frontiersman in
the mid–eighteen hundreds. Before that, the West was considered unfit for civilized peoples, a desert survivable only by
"savage" natives. Spurred on by the railroads, the discovery
of gold, and the American idea of Manifest Destiny, families
began to make their way westward, and the cowboy became
an integral part of life out there.

As more of our country became urbanized in the last century and more farmland got swallowed up, the individual
cowboy faded from American life. It has lived on through
images like the Marlboro Man, country singers in cowboy
hats, and actors like John Wayne. All the while the working cowboy faded to the background, almost to the world of
myth. Though they still serve an essential need on ranches
and farms, the number of workers we would still call "cowboys" has sunk below ten thousand. However, the culture
of the cowboy is still alive in places like Utah, Kansas, and
Texas, and through rodeos, fashion, and craftsmen like
Wilson Capron, who keep these aspects of American culture
and history thriving.

Wilson had reverence for his craft but also an energy
that rubbed off on me. Though committed, he didn't take
it all so seriously that the pleasure drained away. On the
day I worked in his shop, he wore a red-and-white polka-dot

welding cap—the caps also come in striped or flowered patterns. I think the point is that it allows welders to incorporate a little style into their normal safety attire. For Wilson—and for me—it made everything a little looser and more fun.

Though engraving continues to elude my grasp, I *was* in a metal shop, which meant I had some comfort level. I pitched in as we lit up the forge and put in the spur band, a thin piece of metal that becomes the U-shaped part of the spur. Once it was hot and malleable, we moved it to the jig to work the shape into a bend so it could wrap around the heel.

Wilson then sandblasted out the dark gray firescale on the metal before squaring the band's sides with a disc sander. Afterward we welded on the shank, the piece that sticks out the back (where the rowel will attach), drilled a hole for the pin to hold the rowel, then slotted in and welded in the pin. To create the rowel, Wilson started by cutting off a round sliver of metal. Then he cut a center hole and drew on guidelines to split up the diameter like a pizza pie. Wilson then grabbed a farrier's rasp, an aggressive tool that will remove metal fast. The rasp is about fourteen inches long, with a texture that looks like little diamond-shaped teeth on the surface. With the farrier rasp, Wilson hand cut two angles for each "tooth" all the way around the disc. It's difficult, exacting work; the skill comes from keeping consistency all the way around.

While he engraved the rest of the spur, Wilson told me he tends to get "deep into the story" and can spend up to three months on a single set of spurs. I was reminded of David Riccardo, the other metal engraver I worked with, whose faces and figures seemed to be relating a winding and mysterious story that maybe only he knew.

When I asked Wilson my go-to question—Do you consider yourself a craftsman or an artist?—he acknowledged that he wasn't sure what the difference was. "Design has to start somewhere," Wilson said, "and if you don't have good design, which is art, you don't have anything at the end of the day no matter how good your craft is." He has a point: Craft is the execution of an artistic vision. Craft without art will be dull and uninspired; art without craft will be a mess.

Since authentic cowboy culture is sacred to Wilson, he is committed to teaching and sharing his knowledge. For him, the cowboy represents a type of free-spirited elegance, a rugged sophistication. The cowboys of the Old West are part of American history, all of our histories, and if we don't preserve their story, tradition, and work, then we lose part of ourselves.

Wilson also gives back through his part-time teaching, which he understands goes in both directions. Seneca, the ancient Roman philosopher, famously claimed, "While we teach, we learn," and modern science backs him up. Researchers have determined that you learn the most by teaching something. The practice forces you to see your process, to break it down to into parts, and to communicate what you likely do on instinct. I find the same thing in my own work as a metal-shaping teacher. Teaching also gives me exposure to what a beginner thinks and notices. Novices will make a mistake I haven't made in a long time—and it's a challenge for me to help get them out of it. Over time professionals lose that beginner's mind, or *shoshin*, a Zen Buddhist term that nicely captures what teaching can offer the teacher.

Wilson embodies the give-and-take concept because he understands his life is transient. Once he is gone, the craftsman's own identity gets subsumed by what he gives to the world. His work, and the knowledge behind it, will continue to live on.

9: UNDERWATER

When I was twenty-seven, I went on vacation and came back a different person.

My brother and I used to go scuba diving a lot, usually in Lake St. Clair, near our homes in Michigan. But over Thanksgiving in 1998, we took a scuba trip out to Bonaire, in the Caribbean. By the time I came home, though I didn't know it then, my old life would be over.

Even before I was old enough to do it, I'd been attracted to diving. It seemed to hold that perfect amount of adventure and danger. No doubt that some of the allure came from my G.I. Joe action figures with the double scuba tanks and the *Sea Wolf* submarine. I'd take Joe on covert ops missions in our pool.

Once I was finally able to try scuba diving, I discovered how transcendent and gorgeous it is down there. There was this whole world hiding right underneath us. I loved the exploratory nature of diving, the feeling that I was seeing a part of the natural world not available on land: watching a nurse shark in a shallow cave or a collection of seahorses in the wild, spotting octopus, squid, puffer fish, and giant lobsters. There's also the feeling of being in this other world, alien and beautiful, separate from everything you've ever known.

Another draw for scuba diving for me is all the tech: the gear, the gadgets, the knives you need in case you get tangled up in the water or get attacked by a giant squid.

But I haven't been diving in twenty years—not since that trip to Bonaire.

ON THE THIRD day of our trip, our destination was the *Hilma Hooker*, an old drug boat seized by the government. The story is murky, but it either sank or was intentionally sunk to the bottom of the sea in 1984 and is now a popular diving site. The boat is 240 feet long and sits on the seafloor about 100 feet down, between two coral reefs.

Scott and I left before sunrise on a charter boat, which took us out on the water with about twelve other divers. It was a sunny Friday with clear blue skies and a lot of other boats on the water. On deck, I got into my full wet suit, attached all my gear, checked all my gauges, and wiped my mask clean, a routine I had down cold. Stepping off the boat with a giant stride, I hit the water and then tapped my head—signaling to guys up on the boat that I was okay.

But as I was making my descent, something strange happened.

About eighty feet down in the clear blue water, with the wreck in sight, a wave of heat began moving up my body. It started at my feet and slowly drove upward, cycling right up to my head. It was a bizarre sensation, alarming and mysterious.

Then my heart started pounding hard and my breathing became so rapid that I couldn't catch my breath. I had no idea what was going on, but my fight-or-flight reflex kicked in. Hand over hand I started climbing up to the surface, using one of the tag lines that was attached from the sunken ship to a buoy up above.

I broke through the water and reached for our boat, where the dive guys helped me up and took off my gear. As I sat up against the bow, my breathing and heartbeat returned to normal and I slowly regained my composure. But I was pretty badly shaken.

A month or so later, right after the New Year, I was traveling on business for Xerox when it happened again. I had flown to Texas for a work convention. I had just quit smoking the day before and was a little antsy, especially after the long flight from Detroit. As I was checking into my hotel room, I got hit with this strange flare-up, an anxious reaction. On heading into the room with my bags, I started to shake. Then my breathing became accelerated. All of a sudden I was submerged into this nervousness and fear that came out of nowhere. Nothing visible around me was causing it, which somehow made it scarier. Like it was emanating from inside my body.

I sat down on the bed and called my girlfriend back home, who tried to talk me through it. But it was too hard to describe, and talking about it only amplified the feeling, so I hung up and went for a walk. But once I got out among the noise and the crowds, the feeling rose up again. I found my way back to the hotel and lay on my bed, just waiting it out. It eventually subsided, and I made it through the few days of the convention, but the trip—and the return flight, where the feeling returned—were such a disaster that I didn't fly again for five years.

Back in Michigan I started experiencing progressively more intense episodes, which were strange and unnerving. Michigan winters are gloomy and gray anyway, but that winter was emotionally brutal. I went to fewer and fewer places, because everywhere I went seemed to cause an outbreak. I'd be in a work meeting and have to leave, or I'd be on a conference call and have to get up and walk outside, explaining that I needed fresh air. It happened on escalators, on elevators, driving on freeways or stuck in traffic, at the grocery store, at restaurants, even at friends' houses. The weather could bring on an episode, or the temperature, or even a smell in the air. I was a nervous wreck, shaking all the time, afraid to leave the house and, if I did, afraid to be out alone.

It only took a few more weeks before life itself became a trigger. Protecting myself became my only priority, the only thing I even thought about. My life got smaller and smaller, and I consulted doctors, who didn't know what was going on and put me through tests that revealed nothing. I turned to counselors and psychiatrists, and finally I had an explanation. I was experiencing panic attacks, a term I had heard before but didn't really understand. They wanted to put me on medication, which I resisted outright.

The worst part was that the attacks were both unpredictable and inevitable: It was like an invisible force out there that I was sure was coming but also was never sure of when. There was also an element of embarrassment, even shame. I finally found a good psychiatrist whom I connected with. He was a tall, slender man with gray hair and beard and a soft, empathetic voice. No matter how revved up I got in our sessions he remained steady and even. His office was in his home, on the ground floor of a tri-level house in a nice suburban community. The room had a formal air, with a dark green carpet and classic wooden furniture.

As I talked to him, he would run this calming, unobtrusive commentary:

That must have been hard, Eric.

I understand why that was terrifying.

That's interesting. Tell me more about that.

One time, as we were discussing issues I was having at work—because of my attacks—he pulled back the lens in a way I hadn't considered. "Maybe you need to do something different with your life," he said. "Maybe what you're doing now doesn't fulfill you."

"Yeah, maybe," I said. I wasn't mentally there yet. I was just trying to survive each day.

"Well, think about it, Eric. If money didn't matter, if experience didn't matter, if you could do anything, what would you do?"

I didn't even hesitate. "Oh, I'd work with my hands," I said. "Definitely. I'd make things. I enjoy making things. Always have."

"Then that's probably what you should be doing with your life, working with your hands."

"Yeah, maybe," I said.

"What would you make?" he asked.

"Well, I like working with wood. But I love working on bikes. I think I'd like to learn how to build a motorcycle."

"Well maybe that's what you should do, then. How would you do that?"

I was staring out the window.

"Eric?"

"Yep."

"How would you do that?" he asked.

"I don't know."

10: FINDING PEACE

We are born makers. We move what we're learning from our heads to our hearts through our hands.
—BRENÉ BROWN, *author and researcher*

Making things with our hands centers us. The simple action of doing it—of getting lost in it, of shutting everything out until we look up again and realize time has passed—is as close as some of us ever get to that feeling of inner peace. It gives us an opportunity to get away: from our worries, from the regular rhythms of life, even from what we think of as "our minds."

Creation distances us from the world of abstract thought, from blurry guesses about the future and the illusory realness of memories. Our hands ground us, helping us connect—in a physical way—to the here and the now. We escape, not to some far-off place and time, but to the actual present.

When we occupy that headspace, there is a flow that runs through our bodies and minds. Spiritual people call it a state of Zen, and I certainly find a religious aspect to it. When we focus on nothing but our breathing, we become one with it. Working with our hands echoes this experience. We merge with the tools and the process, and we and it become a single undivided thing. Even if the work itself is complicated, there's a simplicity to the process, and a finality to being done: We can see it and we can hold it. What's in front of us matches the picture we had in our mind—or as close as it will get.

> **There are things in your blood that you have**
> **to do, and you have to take care of it.**
> —MAPLE SMITH, *spinner*

MY MOM HAD a craft area in our basement when I was growing up. It was a small space, basically a closet that was turned into a work area with a desk and a sewing machine. I didn't know how to sew, but I enjoyed looking through all the patterns and materials, the strange tools she kept in a rusted old coffee can, the odd scissors with a jagged edge like a wave.

After I started building motorcycles, my mother used to tell people she didn't know where I got my ingenuity. But I know a big part of it came from her. She was an imaginative and creative person who loved making things: needlepoint and crochet, wreaths and bows, plant arrangements, decoupage. She never completely immersed herself in it, especially as the family grew and the pressures of life increased. But when she did take the time, she was never afraid to try something new. For my mom, it never seemed to be about the object itself but more about the feeling of being free to explore what was in her mind. She found peace in the act of creation itself.

I thought about my mother when I met Maple Smith, who for thirty-seven years has lived on an alpaca farm in Central Michigan. With a warm smile and a playful sense of humor, Maple had been many things in her life—painter, potter, horseback riding instructor, schoolteacher—before she discovered spinning yarn and knitting. One day, at an alpaca show with her late husband, she laid eyes on one for the first time and she *knew*.

She had zero experience with the animal, or with spinning or knitting, but she wanted—needed—to have them in her life. She described it as an "inner feeling, a gut reaction" that she had to be near them. The peaceful animal transmitted an aura and an energy as clearly as if it had spoken directly to her. It's powerful to be drawn to something you know nothing about, and Maple chased after it. She brought one home to raise, and that laid the groundwork for the next phase of her life.

Twenty years later, Maple is still raising alpacas, which come in two breeds, each with a different textured fleece:

Huacaya (pronounced *wa-kaya*) and Suri alpacas. Every spring she shears the animals, washes (and sometimes dyes) their fleece, and then spins the fiber into yarn. Though she doesn't breed them anymore, taking care of alpacas keeps her "young and up in the morning," as she said. Caring for them is not just something she does; it is intimately tied to her purpose, to who she is as a person.

Freezing that day on her farm when we filmed her episode, my fingers and toes too numb to feel, I was struck by the strong connection between Maple and her animals. Alpacas are interesting-looking animals; they have a sheep's friendly face, but with an underbite, a smushed face and wide eyes, a long neck, and tall, skinny legs. They struck me as a peaceful animal, with a kind of relaxed happiness. Maple was so affectionate with them, and up close I could feel that magnetism she is so drawn to. Looking into their eyes reminded me of my dog, Buddy, and how it seems as if I can see into his soul.

THE CRAFT OF yarn spinning has been around for ten thousand years. It was originally done solely by hand, until the invention of the spinning wheel in the Middle Ages in either India or the Middle East. The craft then made its way westward to Europe. In order to use this early spinning wheel, commonly called a great wheel (or walking wheel), the spinners would have to remain standing and continually spin it with their hand. They would stand and push the large stationary wheel into motion while drawing fleece through their fingers, applying tension. This motion of repeatedly pushing the wheel with one hand and drawing with the other produced yarn.

In the sixteenth century, the treadle wheel was invented (which helped wood turners like Alan Hollar) and allowed spinners to sit and use their feet so both hands could remain free. Though there have been updated mechanics over time and various styles developed in different regions of the world, the basic principles of spinning haven't changed.

Mahatma Gandhi, who has long been viewed as the very personification of peace, famously took up spinning while imprisoned by the British in the early 1930s. His *charkha*, a type of portable spinning wheel, became an object of deep reverence in the Indian community. It also became a symbol and political statement: The nationalist movement encouraged Indians to make their own items instead of purchasing goods from their British colonizers. Consequently, the spinning wheel became intimately tied with India's push for independence as well as with the nonviolent teachings of the movement's leader. A photograph taken of Gandhi next to his spinning wheel became an iconic image after his death, and he is still associated with the craft.

When I arrived at Maple's alpaca farm, I didn't even know the difference between fleece and yarn, one of the many things Maple kindly explained to me that day. Each time she did it without judgment, in a way that drew me in, which is the sign of a good teacher. She had such a welcoming manner that I came to enjoy the way she'd say, "No, Eric," coating it in a light laugh every time.

The spinning wheel in Maple's house was a treadle wheel from New Zealand. Besides the pedals, which maintain the wheel's spinning motion, the main pieces are the flyer and the bobbin. The flyer is the U-shaped part where the fleece is threaded, and the bobbin (along with the whorl) is the part that spins. The yarn spinner uses both feet to keep the bobbin spinning at an even speed. It's like pedaling a bike, with your feet alternating between the downswing and the upswing. The circular movement (called a "cam motion") is used to create something linear, which in this case is yarn.

The spinning wheel has a distinct sound, quiet but constant. The challenge is to lock in and get the pace going at a consistent speed while also using tension in your hands to pull the material being spun. When I sat down to try it, having never done it in my life, it took me some time to find that cadence. As you draw the yarn out, your grip shouldn't be about force. It's more about guiding it, even letting it go, rather than pulling it to your will. You have to become at one with it, accept what it's there to do and what you're there to help it do. And once you lock in—to the wheel's recurring pitch, and the repetition of the movement—it's an enormously peaceful process.

Spinning the wheel properly relies on muscle memory, a term that we use all the time but is worth thinking about: The body has its own memory. When a professional basketball player shoots a free throw or a black belt blocks a kick, they're operating from muscle memory. Our body internalizes the movement and retains the action in a way that our conscious brain may not even be aware of.

There was a famous patient in the 1950s, known as H.M., who suffered from such debilitating seizures that doctors sliced away the part of his brain that caused them. The seizures stopped, but afterward he was unable to form new memories. He literally couldn't remember things that had happened a few minutes before. However, one ingenious doctor, Brenda Milner, came up with an experiment that showed that his *body* could still retain memory, even if his mind couldn't. For a period of time she asked H.M. every day to try to draw a five-pointed star upside down, in a way that he could only see his work through a mirror. It was difficult, and H.M. had no memory each day that he'd tried it before, but over a few days, he got better and better. It got the point where he could do it easily, and one day he knocked it out immediately. H.M. told Milner he was surprised that he picked it up right away!

Potter David MacDonald called muscle memory "intuitive kinetic knowledge," and it operates as a base to work from when encountering an unfamiliar craft. I had the advantage of years of working with my hands, the muscle memory of how light or hard to press down or grip something, which was useful in spinning yarn. As I got the hang of it, I saw that it wasn't so different from metal work: the hand-eye and muscle coordination required, the technical skill, and the understanding of mechanics overlapped considerably.

The wheel's movement is meditative, and I could've watched Maple carry out that hypnotic motion all day. It was like staring at a fan for so long that the blades merge together into a single object. When I mentioned the appeal of the circular movement, Maple agreed. "Circles are comforting," she said.

Circles are indeed symbolic. They evoke unity, togetherness, and support. The circle has no beginning or ending, no separation between up and down, left and right, no part that is more distinctive than any other. When we join together with others in a way without hierarchy, we form a circle. Each piece is equal; it's a deeply democratic shape. The circle also conjures the continuation of energy, of life, the feeding of something back into itself.

Maple's reciprocal relationship with her alpacas also echoes this idea of the eternal circle. She takes care of the animals, and, in turn, they provide the fleece and her livelihood. The fleece is part of its own natural circle, being shorn in the spring and harvested and transformed into Maple's craft, which goes out into the world. Then the fleece grows back and the cycle begins again. "I give to them and they give to me, and on it goes," she said to me.

Years ago Maple was an elementary school teacher, and now she still enjoys teaching anyone who is interested in learning. Her granddaughters became beneficiaries of her knowledge, having learned spinning at a young age. She smiled as she spoke of how they would tell *their* children how Grandma taught them this craft, how she'll still be there—through the craft—after she is gone. Circles inside circles.

Maple told me that spinning connects her to those in the past, especially women, who have usually been associated with the craft. When she picks up the yarn and holds it in her hands, she can feel their energy. She doesn't quite understand what that is, but she knows it's there. "I like that warm glow I get from carrying on the tradition," she told me.

I thought of all the tools that have made their way through generations. I thought of Walter Arnold, the stone carver who still uses a nineteenth-century chisel given to him by his mentor. I thought of the small ball-peen hammer I got from my dad's father, the band saw from my mom's father, the sockets and wrenches and pliers that my dad has passed down to me through the years. As I've gotten older, I've become conscious of their historical and emotional value, their energy.

The entire experience of yarn spinning was so unfamiliar to me. Unlike metal, strength and power are not part of the equation. Actually, they'll work against you. There's a gentleness and a safety to spinning. Often in my own shop or on the show, it's intense. I'm working with tools, machines, and material that could cause serious damage: cut off a hand, knock out an eye, or blow out someone's hearing. But there was a calm that ran through everything Maple and I did that day, like we were communing with something outside of ourselves, something that was no less real because we couldn't exactly pinpoint what it was or where it came from.

Maple admitted to me that the process meant more to her than the final product, sort of like all my mom's projects. She has gotten to the point where she spins automatically, not even needing to watch what she is doing. Her mind is free to comfortably wander because she is grounded, engaging in something as natural to her as breathing. Maybe it's what she was put on this Earth to do—she certainly thinks so. "There are things in your blood that you have to do," Maple told me, "and you have to take care of it." Knowing what we're here for, and what we must protect, is another way that we can all find peace.

MY DAD STILL has an enviable work ethic, but back when I was growing up even the projects he had going on outside of his regular job—landscaping, painting, window replacement, masonry—always got done. I don't know if he ever found any peace working so much, or if he was even searching for it, but he'd work all week and then spend Saturday and Sunday finishing projects so he could start up another. Slowing down wasn't an option.

It's likely my dad's approach rubbed off on me. But I'm older now and I'm more willing to let go—and to not make my work my burden. It's a never-ending struggle to find that work-life balance. I can't count the number of times I've pushed myself to complete something only to ruin it. I now know I have to walk away sometimes to save it. If I ever brought an efficiency expert into my shop, he'd immediately home in on that habit. But this is how I need to do it: slow down, never rush, and enjoy the process of creating.

When I first started my motorcycle business, I was in the shop seven days a week. But I've mellowed. I'll probably work until I die, so if I don't spend time with my daughter or in the outdoors now, I may never get to. Lately I start the weekend by leaving a little early on a Friday to go fishing. I'll spend two or three days either walking through a stream fly-fishing for trout or taking my sixteen-foot console fishing boat on a lake and casting for bass. I'm drawn to the sport of it, the challenge and the technical aspects that surround it. I'm a catch-and-release guy, and for me it's about mastering the cast, figuring out the strategy of which baits and lures to use, and being able to mimic the bait in a way that will entice the fish. There's nothing like skipping a lure thirty feet and seeing it skitter way underneath the dock and hit the seawall. Although my consistency is lacking, that satisfying motion is the very definition of peace for me.

I know some people enjoy sitting on a boat with a rod and a beer and a far-off stare—but that's not for me. It's not in my nature to just sit and float on the water. For me, peace is when my focus and energy are in harmony with what I'm doing. Our lives, wants, needs are always smacking up against the outside world. Peace is when we find a place, if only briefly, where that tension between us and the world fades. Or maybe it's more accurate to say that the tension doesn't bother us.

Of course, another way I find peace is being out on my motorcycle. A ride gives me the chance to not think about much at all. It's enough just to pay attention to what I'm doing and enjoy how there's nothing directly separating me from the world. My bike is particularly stripped down: no windscreen, radio, or gauges, not even a speedometer.

When I was a kid growing up in Michigan, my family would go on Sunday drives after church down by Lake St. Clair along Lake Shore Road in Gross Pointe. The drives had no destination or endpoint and they were usually my mom's idea, a way to spend time together. I'm sure those excursions made my dad nuts—he is not a meander kind of guy. And as for me, in the backseat, I had a feeling of being locked out from the world.

A hundred years ago when the Model T first became popular, at the infancy of mass production, cars were boisterous-sounding machines. Since the frames were up on skinny tires, the vehicle responded to every alteration in the road, which were not the sleek, paved things we know of today. The car's four-cylinder motor roared like a big lawn mower engine. The mixing of fuel and pulling in air through a tight spot made a loud *pop pop pop pop* sound. Without an overstuffed muffler, the sound of the exhaust leaving the car was pronounced, and the windows didn't offer any noise separation. The driver felt resistance in the accelerator because of the mechanical linkage between the pedal and the carburetor. There was no power steering, which created instant feedback between driver and steering wheel and wheels and road. The whole experience produced a connection: between your body, the car, the terrain, and the motion. It was unmistakable.

On my bike I get the visceral feeling of being on a machine. I can sense that five inches of space between my boots and the cement, how I'm close enough to drag my foot. Every divot and pebble I touch on the road I can feel through the bars: A palpable, direct line runs from the wheels to the machine to my body. There's a resistance on my throttle and I can feel the tension of that carburetor spring as I twitch that cable, the force of the clutch pack when I squeeze the lever. The wind is beating on my face and pushing me back, and I can hear the sound of the valve train smacking around.

My Harley is an older model, and it's very loud and mechanical-sounding. People who are used to riding newer bikes get alarmed, fearing that something's really wrong with the bike—but that's just how it sounds. I take comfort in knowing what it all means. Often, in language, we conflate peace and quiet—*I just need some peace and quiet*—but for me, total quiet is undesirable. The noise of my bike is the purest kind of peace I know.

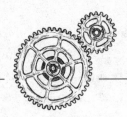

11: DISCOVERY

Messes are the artist's true friend . . . we need to make messes in order to find out who we are and why we are here. —ANNE LAMOTT

Before my daughter could even talk it was obvious that she had a creative mind. She and I have been coloring, cutting, gluing, drawing, and painting together for as far back as I can remember. Some projects don't go as well as planned, like the time we made Christmas ornaments with glitter and I spent the holidays getting it out of every crevice of the house. But I can embrace a worthy mess as much as anyone. I know it's for a good reason—that's how she's going to learn, using her hands and getting inside all that chaos. For a kid that's a rite of passage.

Last year, when she was in eighth grade, she asked me for any leather I had lying around at the shop, and when

I went to her pick her up from her mom's, she showed me what she had created: leather saddles and harnesses for her Breyer horse models. After watching some YouTube videos, she figured out how to do it on her own. Through the years she's made pillows and ornaments and, for a while, dragons out of oven-bake clay. She'd then paint them, and add glitter, of course. Always with the glitter.

My daughter is a talented artist and an incredible drawer, but as she gets older, the challenge is to hold on to that creative impulse, to ensure it doesn't get completely drowned out by the rest of life. When we are creative, we are tapping in to the younger and more idealistic version of ourselves. The one that doesn't care if it's any good, if we know what we're doing, who's going to see it, what their response will be, and how we're going to feel about that response. That openness is part of being alive.

All kids are natural artists and craftsmen—building forts out of pillows, making daisy chains with construction paper, painting cardboard boxes into spaceships. Childhood is made up of hours of planning and improvising, hypothesis and testing, trial and error to figure out what works and what doesn't. Over time, a confidence develops from that kind of playing around, a mastery over one little part of the world.

Children don't just decide one day to stop being creative. We casually say they "grow out of it"—like candy or temper tantrums or Santa Claus—as though it were inevitable. I'd argue that a contributing factor is us: The adult world doesn't value this kind of imagination. We stop encouraging it, and even start to look down on it.

A few weekends ago my daughter and I were sitting around the house. The TV was on, just as background noise, and I was working on carving a wooden cross, something I've been doing a lot lately. She was sitting on the couch next to me, scrolling through Pinterest on her phone, which I know a lot of fourteen-year-olds spend their weekend doing.

"What are you doing now?" I asked.

"What do you mean?" She turned her phone outward to show me what she was looking at.

"No, I mean creatively, what are you doing lately?" I realized I hadn't seen her drawing or making anything lately.

"Nothing," she said, shrugging me off a bit.

"Well, why not?"

"I don't really have anything to work on."

She knew I wasn't going to let that pass. "How about you find something to learn, then?" I asked. "Instead of looking at pictures of what other people made, how come you're not making things yourself?"

"I don't know."

"You want to learn how to carve?" I gestured to the cross and all the knives I had out.

"Nah, not really."

"Well, what about something like knitting?"

"Yeah," she said, making a face like *no*. "I don't know."

"Come on, there's got to be something," I said. "Decide what you want to learn and we'll go get what you need. You want to make a model? You want to paint? Whatever you want."

She looked at me and shrugged her shoulders. "I sort of want to learn calligraphy," she said.

"All right, great! Let's go," I said, slapping my hands together and getting up. "Let's do it." We shut off the TV and went to Michaels, where I bought her different brush pens and an instructional book on beginner's calligraphy.

On the ride back to the house, I turned to her. "Listen," I said, "I know you have all these other things going on in your life, but I don't want you lose your drive to create. I want you to learn stuff. You're not going to be good at it at first. It takes time."

"I know," she said, and I got the feeling that she did. I'm always saying 90 percent is easy; it's the last 10 percent that counts. I'm sure she's internalized that—maybe she's even sick of hearing it.

What came of it, whether she stuck with the calligraphy or moved on to something else, was not important. It was about the *stepping in*. I want her to flex that muscle. As adults we often abandon the willingness to try. Some of it is ego—we don't want to be beginners—and some of it is priorities. If you ask an adult what they want to learn, they'll tell you. Almost everyone has *something* they've always wanted to try. But if you poke further, into the practical details of getting started, you run up against a wall of commitments they can't or won't shift around. That roadblock just sits there, stubborn and immovable. For years. Or a lifetime.

Making things is putting ourselves out there in a naked and vulnerable way. I think it's fear: fear of exposing ourselves, fear of not being good at something, fear of revealing our imperfections. But the imperfections are where the value is. They speak to our humanness.

Social media—where we are all increasingly spending our time—plays a part in this insecurity. Our Facebook and Instagram pages are curating exercises, and dishonest ones at that. We're editing our lives to present the best version of ourselves, filtering it in a way that it shines abnormally bright and removes all the flaws. Our online selves create the illusion that we don't have any of those; because others don't show theirs, we are engaged in an arms race of impossible standards. I'm no different. When I take a picture of something I'm working on in the shop, before I post it on social media, I spend time considering if it's good enough to make public.

If we tell ourselves we can't do it because we don't know how, that assumption only solidifies the older we get. It will become more stubbornly embedded in our thinking. Whether we are planing wood or baking cakes, we have to be willing to go through a learning curve. We need to do it poorly and incorrectly and sloppily and then learn how and why it turned out that way. We need to make a mess of things.

As the father of a teenager, it bothers me that schools have been reducing the classes that bring out that side of kids: arts, music, and vocational training. Those classes develop our imaginations, teach us problem solving, instill confidence, and imbue us with a respect for tools and the process. Whether it's a custom bike or a papier-mâché mask, there's an undeniable sense of pride when you make something on your own. I know the practical reasons why schools have cut back on these classes—budget shortfalls, for one— but it feels like we're sacrificing too much.

If it continues in this direction, each passing generation is going to lose these necessary skills that help them figure out the world and make sense of who they are. You might not have to work on your own car one day, and chances are very slim you'll ever get paid to play an instrument, but shouldn't you be given the opportunity to discover what those things have to offer? Can we expand the idea of education beyond the narrow boxes it's stuck in?

"You have to make the mistakes," Shawn Messenger, a glassblower I worked with on *A Craftsman's Legacy*, told me in her glass studio. "And sometimes the mistakes are better than what you thought it was going to be like. If you don't fail, you're probably going to be bored by what you do."

I'm always looking for new things to fail at. Bring it on.

Just about anything can be fixed.
—NATHAN BOWER, *clockmaker*

I'M A MECHANICALLY-MINDED person who lives for gears and gadgets, and I spent two days with clockmaker Nathan Bower up close and asking questions, but I'm *still* not certain how a clock works. The whole process is incredibly mysterious to me. It comes down to a pendulum, springs, and a gear set. The pendulum, which has a specific weight, provides the initial motion; its momentum, maintained by gravity, triggers the mechanism, which is a series of gears. A clockmaker uses three gear sets, each one based on a unit of time: seconds, minutes, or hours. One gear moves a certain amount at a certain speed, which sets off the next, which starts the next.

As a clockmaker, Nathan's work requires a level of exactitude and attention to detail that stands out, even among the most impressive people we have featured on the show. When Nathan started out he had no background or lineage in the craft of clockmaking at all—his parents are children's book authors. He simply made a decision to learn this incredibly difficult and technical skill. When he was eleven years old, he took on his first broken clock in his home. Sitting down with it, he fixed it in the most straightforward way possible: he took it apart and put it back together. Twenty years later, in his parents' house, that clock continues to run.

The first mechanical clockmakers in Europe were medieval monks who needed a way of marking when to call people to prayer. It was not until the Industrial Revolution, when trains were able to shuttle people from place to place, that an agreed-upon time standard became necessary. By the twentieth century, when factories and mass-produced parts came along, the individual clockmaker became less necessary, though the rich and complicated craft lives on in people like Nathan Bower.

After fixing clocks for ten years Nathan began to create his own clocks, which are astounding works of art. He makes skeleton clocks, which are transparent, with all the gears exposed. You can literally see what makes it tick. There is a beauty in opening up a machine to the world like that, to show how it operates. So many machines nowadays hide the works; you couldn't figure out how they operate, or how to fix them, even if you wanted to.

Cars were once relatively easy to fix yourself. You could take the vital organs out—the carburetor or distributor—and clean a clogged part or replace a worn part, and it would run again. But mass manufacturing has removed us even further from understanding how things work. A lot of it is about profits: We can't fix things ourselves if we don't know how they're made. Eleven-year-old Nathan Bower knew this, and that one formative experience sent him down the rabbit hole to learn how to put these machines together.

In Nathan's workshop, surrounded by his complicated and intricate clocks, I got lost thinking about the great invisible force of time. It is one of those things we are all ruled by, yet I had rarely stopped and thought about the literalness of the clock: its connection to the Earth's rotation around the sun, that direct line to nature, and the fact that the divisions of time really only exist for people. The moving gears are a physical reminder of our presence here on Earth, of the time that is inescapably—click after click—moving forward for all of us.

Something I respected about Nathan is that he was open to talking about how his journey wasn't a straight line, how much he failed when he was starting out. It's so important to push against our comfort zone. We grow by stretching ourselves, by opening ourselves up and making room for new knowledge.

Nathan spoke to me about the richness and value of failure, how maybe we're not really built to learn from success.

Our minds do not glom onto it in the way that they do with failure. Of course ruminating isn't good for us, but getting comfortable with what failure has to offer is enormously valuable.

Over time, those failures have produced something considerable in Nathan; his mechanical ingenuity is off the charts. If he needs a certain tool that doesn't exist or is hard to get, he just makes it on his own. For instance, a while back, in order to cut a clock's gears, he needed a very specific type of indexing plate. So he made one himself and attached it to his metal lathe. Nathan's indexing plate was a thin round piece of steel that had a number of small holes in it, creating a circle, with each hole corresponding to a specific measurement. The indexing plate advances the gear a specific amount and allows him to cut in a preset, circular pattern. To make something as exacting as an indexing plate, you have to have such trust in your hand-eye movement, your patience, and your attention to detail. It's like making a sophisticated ruler; if you're off by even the tiniest amount, everything you make while using it will be too.

Nathan's gears are aesthetically beautiful as well as functional. Once the gear itself is cut, he hand cuts the decorative webbing inside the gears with a jeweler saw, which is a small handsaw with a very taut and fine blade. The blades are so thin that any incorrect motion on your part will break the blade: Too much pressure, not enough pressure, angling your hand incorrectly, will all cause it to break.

Nathan showed me a clock that he built for an art competition, which took him nine months and used 180 individual parts. (He won.) Despite that, the style is minimalistic, everything unnecessary removed. The whole piece has an airy feel, as Nathan leaves gaps to punctuate what he has left in.

The clockmaker, the clock, and time itself all represent the idea of patience. I picture those tinkerers in ancient Egypt and China who tried to get the shadow of the sun on dirt or the flow of water to match up with the Earth's turning. I'm in awe of how long that process must have taken. But people began to figure it out because they sensed, maybe not consciously, that civilization couldn't progress without it. Each innovator had to put in the work that would allow the next innovator to pick up and run with it. They knew that discovery is a long, painstaking process. It's like the slow, deliberate exposure of a photograph, taking its time to reveal itself.

Nowadays clocks are so omnipresent that we don't even think about them. They're on phones, dashboards, microwave ovens, banks, computers, and billboards. It's strange: Time is so important in our lives—maybe the most important thing—but there are so few people who can make or fix an actual clock. Nathan told me when he was first starting out he got hired immediately at a jewelry shop because they couldn't find anyone who could fix clocks. It is a trade that is dying so rapidly, yet it is so essential to our society.

Time is both the invisible force that we are all bound to and a man-made scaffolding that helps us navigate our world. You could argue that managing time, understanding how we use the time we are given, is one of the great challenges of life. I feel as though the clockmaker is intimately connected to these ideas, that he has his hands on the pulse of something so essential in what it means to be human.

OPENNESS ALSO MEANS a willingness to improvise, to listen, to be flexible, to let yourself be open to discovery. Craftsmen regularly talk about figuring out what the piece "wants" to be or which way the material "wants" to go, and I know exactly what they mean. It's not just executing a plan, imposing your will on something, which is a one-way relationship. It's more like a back-and-forth conversation.

A craftsman might have a projection of what something will be, but as he gets into the work, the material itself might alter the plans. If he's turning wood, the material may open up a little bit, allowing him to see something in the wood that wasn't on the surface, like maybe the grain is more exposed, and he might adjust his design to bring that out. The material itself is not just a passive receptacle of a craftsman's ideas. It has a say too.

Whether it's wood, metal, or glass, there is going to be value hidden inside it somewhere; its full character isn't always immediately visible or obvious. It's no different from people—how they seem to be one thing in an initial encounter but layers get revealed as you get to know them. When I begin building a motorcycle, I don't have a clear blueprint of exactly what it will be. I have some plan, but I'm always open to an opportunity to improve on it. There's an element of artistry to it.

A customer of mine, an eccentric guy with unique taste, recently brought in a bike that I originally built for him in 2003. He was interested in a total transformation and asked me to completely redesign the bike—basically, he wanted me to give the bike a new personality. I always say that a bike should match the rider, and he's a different person than he was fourteen years ago, so it made sense that he wanted the bike to evolve along with him.

In the shop I spent a lot of time looking at his old bike, playing with designs and updates in my head, envisioning where the piece was going to start, where it was going to stop, how we were going to mount it. A bike should emerge organically from the process: what color it wants to be, what additional details it gets, what changes I make or don't make.

A set of handlebars, for instance, is almost like a bike's face. They can completely change how a bike looks, and how the rider looks on it, because the handlebars alter the rider's position. One set of handlebars can give the bike an easygoing style while another can make that exact same bike look very aggressive. The handlebars allow the rider to control the bike, but the design of them will also dictate how well the rider will enjoy the ride. A set of handlebars can look great and be miserable to use.

Back in 2003, this customer was a lot more specific about what kind of bike he wanted, but this time around he was more open to my suggestions. That willingness to let go is something that might have come with age and experience. It's possible he had become more like that in the rest of his life too. He even was willing to forego one of the few things he came in wanting for sure: a specific type of oil tank, which was two growler-sized beer kegs welded together. It was a clever idea, but once it was done, it just didn't work. To his credit, he let me try again—with something simpler—and ended up agreeing with my less-is-more philosophy.

This kind of openness also leaves room for lucky accidents, for stumbling into discoveries. Early in the process, after I put on the new front end, I took a picture of the bike in my shop and sent it to the client. In the photograph, there was another bike directly behind it, and the resulting picture—which collapsed the depth and merged the two—gave me an idea. The frame of the "Frankenbike" had an arched backbone and projected an entirely new tank line—which I ended up mimicking.

The final bike that emerged was inspired by the Mad Max movies, which take place in a dystopian future where the weapons and vehicles are all scrounged together from the scraps that are left lying around. The bike is minimalist, with few extraneous items. A lot of the time manufacturers hide the mechanics of something when I feel like the beauty is in the design of the mechanics, like with Nathan's skeleton clocks.

The bike is a clash of different styles—BMX dirt bike–type influence, '60s/'70s chopper influence, an older shovelhead engine but a modern transmission, knobby tires, and motocross type wheels (light aluminum with spokes). The pieces came together to form a true original and gave the bike an unconventional persona, like wearing a tuxedo jacket with jeans, something I have been known to do. There is no way I could have sketched it out in advance if I'd had to. I needed to work my way through it to discover what it was going to be.

Because of my commitment to discovery, I don't do sketches up front for clients. In my earlier days, because I can't draw, I had a guy who would sketch out my projects. If a client wanted to hire me, I'd describe my ideas to the illustrator and he'd draw it and we'd go back and forth, like a witness with a police sketch artist. Before any tradesman builds a reputation, people aren't going to just hand him thousands of dollars, or their beloved bike.

My main issue was that those sketches locked me in; I *had to* build what was drawn for the client, because that's what they paid for. If I wanted to make changes I'd have to go to clients and try to convince them why I thought we should go in a different direction. Sometimes I could articulate what I wanted to do or why, but other times it was more feel, instinct, and other things that don't always translate well into words.

"Well, what about the drawing?" they'd ask.

And I'd answer with some version of "Yeah, it looks good on paper, but I don't think it's going to work in metal."

As soon as I reached the point that I could get away with it, I told potential clients that I didn't do drawings—they would just have to trust me.

Sometimes I come up with an idea for a bike that I have no idea how to pull off. When this happens, I break it down, almost in reverse: From the final idea to the single piece, I tear it down to the most basic point, to where I know what I'm doing. Then I build forward from there, one step at a time, figuring it out as I go. You can get all the way to the end doing it that way.

The satisfaction comes from ending up in a place that I might not have been able to get to if I were too rigid in thought and planning. In one episode of *A Craftsman's Legacy* I met with a rocking horse maker named Jackie Wilson. She articulated this concept perfectly, and her words still echo around in my head: "I'm always trying to find if there's a better way to do it than I'm doing it."

12: TRADITION

**The best way to understand craft, I believe, is to
think of it as a conversation flowing through time.**
—PETER KORN, *furniture maker and author*

Whether we are conscious of it or not, we are always surrounded by the past. Our world is comprised of objects that came from the time, innovation, and hard work of people who were here before us. The chair and desk you are sitting at, the lightbulb shining on that desk, the glass window that's insulating the outdoors, the book in your spouse's lap, the leather of this chair, the coffee in that cup, and the cup itself. History is living and breathing and right in front of our eyes. We just have to choose to see it.

One of the ways cultures try to tap into our collective memory is through tradition, the bridge that merges the past, present, and even the future. It is how the dead speak to us, and how we communicate across the divides of space and time. It is the remedy for a disposable age.

I believe that craftsmen are a little more plugged in to the backstory, the traditions of all things. The past hovers over us, acting as a guide and a template—sometimes for how to do things, sometimes for how *not* to do things. That's partly why the apprentice-mentor relationship is so important. And it's not just about the what, but the *how*. And the how is often multidimensional, requiring interaction with a human being. There is an oral aspect to the tradition that requires a relationship, a bond that goes both ways.

Modern Europeans have maintained an especially high appreciation for craftsmen and the programs to train them. I have a friend from England who decided as a young man he wanted to be a metal shaper—what the British call a "panel beater"—and he went through a stringent apprenticeship program. For a prescribed amount of time he just did metal filing, then he'd only work the wheel, then only weld, then only use the shot or sandbag to strike into the metal. Over time, through this deliberate process, step by step, skill by skill, he became a well-rounded shaper.

Germany's apprentice system is among the most involved. The country has an education structure where it splits off at a certain point: Some kids feed into the university system and the others feed into trade study. But it's not hierarchical like it is in the States—like white collar versus blue collar and all the socioeconomic associations that come with those labels. Both kinds of workers are able to make a good living, and they are treated equally. Germany is a thriving modern economy where you can live on a middle-class income from trade work as comfortably as anyone with a college degree can. Close to 60 percent of those starting out in Germany begin as apprentices in all kinds of fields.

European countries far surpass the United States in the amount and kinds of apprenticeships, and according to a recent article in the *Washington Post*, "it's not unusual to find top executives of companies who started as apprentices." The system has worked for centuries, and by keeping it in place and adapting it to new trades, the craftsmen tradition there has naturally moved into the twenty-first century.

The closest thing we have in the States to European-style apprenticeships is the journeyman system in the trades, which is a way of learning on the job. ("Journeyman" is from the French word for "day," *journée*.) Apprenticeships are far rarer in this country, by an enormous margin. Only around 5 percent of people entering the workforce begin as apprentices (though this doesn't account for unpaid internships), and it's formalized for only a few occupations, like plumbers and machinists.

Despite this lack of infrastructure, the craftsman culture has managed to survive in America, but along its own stream. Because of its separateness, craftsmen hold tightly to the traditions that inform and shape their work.

> **The frustrating part for me is
> I only have one lifetime to learn it all.**
> —KEVIN CASHEN, *bladesmith*

IT'S FASCINATING TO think about how we are living someone else's ancient history. Hundreds, maybe thousands, of years from now people will be studying the culture, inventions, influencers, and key moments of our time. The ancient Greeks and Romans couldn't have known what parts of their society would last and what wouldn't, what aspects would become building blocks for our civilization and what would be mostly lost to history. What drove them was what motivates so many of us: the desire and responsibility to leave some kind of positive mark. Something that proclaims: *We were here.*

Bladesmith Kevin Cashen is one of a handful of people working to keep swordsmithing alive in the Western world.* When I met Kevin in his shop in rural Michigan, he talked passionately about how worlds once rose and fell on the shoulders of swordsmiths.

Swords were the foundation of past empires, and the quality of a people's swords meant life or death. If the swords were not up to par, or even if they were weaker than the opposing army's, their lives would crumble. If the enemy figured out a better way to forge their swords, a stronger metallurgy, that was it. We wouldn't be reading about them in our textbooks thousands of years later. The swordsmiths were once the last line of defense in protecting empires. Now they are our last line of defense from this craft being completely lost to history.

KNOWN AS "Queen of the Weapons," swords evolved out of shorter daggers from the Neolithic era (10,000–5,000 B.C.), which were made from flint, ivory, or bone. The

---

* It's swordsmith, not swordmaker, because he literally creates the metal.

history of the sword is essentially the history of metal. With the discovery of how to make metal—and the technology to manipulate that metal—larger and more lethal weapons became possible. Copper knives were elongated into copper swords, which were pretty flimsy. The first bronze swords became common around 2300 B.C., in the Aegean area of Turkey and Greece. Once the metal became stronger, the swords could be longer and more effective for close combat. The sword's metal had to be strong, but it also couldn't be so brittle that it would break, so a certain amount of flexibility was required. Finding this balance became one of the sword-smith's main challenges.

Stronger swords made of iron first appeared around the twelfth century B.C. When early smelters accidentally left iron in the charcoal longer than normal, they discovered steel. (Steel is essentially iron plus carbon.) The first steel swords showed up in China and India around the fifth century B.C. and then expanded around the ancient world, with each civilization—including the ancient Greeks, Persians, and Romans—putting their own spin on them. The Romans' popular gladius sword "conquered the known world," Kevin explained, and it laid the groundwork for centuries of European swords.

As with most inventions, swords developed and improved out of necessity, as armies were looking for stronger swords to fight their battles, which were as constant a part of life back then as going to work and spending time with your family. Weapons were so central to early civilizations that "whole cultures grew up around where the richest metallic ore deposits could be found," as Kevin's website notes. In the Western world, steel came directly from raw ore until the sixteenth century A.D., with the introduction of the blast furnace.

The actual tracing of the sword's history is complicated because it's not a straight line, and swords in the East—China and Japan—had their own progression separate from that of the Western world. For instance, Japanese swords date back to the third century A.D., and the distinctive curved Japanese swords (like the *katana*, used by samurai) were produced in the eighth century to help the riders who fought on horseback. Various style and design features developed in these countries, but a complete understanding of how they were made has vanished with history. Once firearms came along, starting in the Ottoman Empire around the fifteenth century, swords slowly faded out of the picture. As guns progressively improved with each century, the sword fell out of favor, though the allure of swords has never really died.

Swordmaking today is most associated with Eastern cultures, because that side of the world has upheld the traditions. In Asia there are still families of master swordsmiths with direct lineage to those from centuries ago. "Eastern cultures revered the sword as an object in a different way than the Western culture did," Kevin Cashen told me.

Unfortunately, in the West, the craft has faded away. Kevin uses terms like "lost art" and "dead craft" to describe what he does, but the purpose of his work is actually ensuring that those descriptions are not true. One thing that helped breathe new life into the swordmaking tradition in the West was that after World War II many veterans brought back Japanese swords like *katanas* to the States. People were fascinated with these works of craftsmanship, which caused a spike of interest in them.

Swords are one of those objects that conjure ideas of romance and fantasy, along with this childlike wonder that still lingers inside me. I used to play with swords and shields when I was a kid, pretending to be a knight or looking for monsters in the basement. I remember my dad turned an old piece of wood paneling into a shield, put a cabinet door handle on the back, and wrote a giant *E* in wide blue Magic Marker on the face. Then he made me a simple sword out of pinewood with a hilt (which includes both the handle and the crosspiece above it). I spent hours playing with those, imagining myself in deadly battles and precarious escapes. Working with Kevin was like stepping into one of those old contests from my youth.

In order to become a swordsmith, Kevin had to be something of a Renaissance man: equal parts historian, artist, scientist, mathematician, and detective. Some of his replica swords are not just visual copies; they are authentically produced with metals that are scientifically accurate to their era. He will replicate the ancient process by digging his own ore out of the ground and smelting his own iron in a bloomery, a type of early charcoal furnace.

History is not just the final object but the steps and the processes that lead to it. The further back you go, the harder this is to know, to preserve, and to teach. Kevin has to get *inside* the swords. His historically accurate blades have very specific properties, including carbon distribution that matches the historical period in which they originated, whether that's ancient Rome or sixteenth-century Saxony. So part of his work is investigating the molecular structure of the metal and understanding the carbon deposits within that metal. The carbon in modern steel is exceptionally well homogenized, meaning evenly spread out. But in earlier eras, swordsmiths hadn't perfected that process. The carbon back then was scattered and patchy, with soft and hard dispersed throughout the sword's metal.

For Kevin the past is a deep well, but some of it remains in darkness; he has to piece aspects together from available clues. As he evolved in his understanding of swordsmithing, he has plunged deeper into the craft's history and chemistry. One of Kevin's most fascinating projects has been working with scientists to figure out one of the great sword mysteries in history: the Vikings' Ulfberht sword.

The Vikings developed a type of steel that was so well homogenized that its strength was far superior to any other steels of the time. Carbon content is the difference between steel and iron, but if that carbon is not equally spread out, the swords are flimsy and unreliable. This is what was common during these times—steel with chunks of carbon here and there. The Vikings were somehow able to develop a better process, but because the Vikings were nomadic and conquered other peoples over vast distances, their records are nonexistent or confusing, so re-creating their process was extremely difficult.

Their heavy reliance on trading also made it difficult to decipher exactly where things originated. It's very possible the Vikings learned their swordmaking technique from a culture that has been entirely lost to history. Some civilizations, or at least their inventions, have indeed fallen through this black hole. They'd have a run of progress and innovation, but then they'd get conquered, and all their technology would disappear. Then a hundred years later they'd discover the same things all over again—or different versions of them.

Archeologists can now find an artifact, carbon-date it, and find out where and when it came from. But something that is so much harder to determine is *how* it was originally made. We hypothesize, theorize, and fill in the blanks. But the true root of it—the *story* of it—is gone forever. Kevin told me that even if he's making something like a Revolutionary War sword, which is really not that long ago, he mostly has to rely on drawings and paintings to figure it out.

Kevin's job is basically to reverse engineer history. I've said that nobody is doing anything mystical in these workshops, but Kevin comes as close as anyone I've met so far. In fact, when I used the word "alchemy" to describe the work of early swordsmiths, Kevin got excited. "I can't believe you used that word!" he said. "That's exactly what it was." He talked about how all the alchemists back then were actually phonies and charlatans. But the lonely guy down the road figuring out how to move the atoms in metal through fire? *That* was the real alchemist.

Another element that makes Kevin's job especially difficult is that he works on his own. In earlier times, a variety of different craftsmen came together to make the swords in order to consistently supply the armies. There was the blacksmith, who dealt with the metal, the craftsman who just did the hilt, and the craftsman who just did the handle decoration, along with battle sword specialists and parade sword specialists. It was essentially sword by committee. But Kevin has to juggle all of it. When he comes across a sword he wants to replicate, he might have to invest *two years* to learn a specific skill that it requires. Kevin once worked for five years with a client who wanted a certain twelfth-century sword re-created.

On the day I visited Kevin, we made a spatha sword, which dates to first-century Rome and was once used in gladiator fights and in battles. The sword is made up of two large parts: There's the blade and there's the hilt, which consists of the guard—so the other person doesn't slice your hand off—the grip, and the pommel, which keeps your hand from slipping off.

Kevin's workshop is a combination of a smithy, a metal shop, and a laboratory. It's filled with old equipment, things you'd see in an old university lab, like microscopes and X-ray machines, so Kevin can examine the molecular content of the metal. He sought out these outdated machines that companies would have probably scrapped, but which work perfectly for his purposes.

Though Kevin knows how the process works, better than just about anyone, he still carries a sense of wonder for the sword and its long tradition. He told me he's still in awe that he can make "steel from rocks, digging it out of the ground . . . smelting your own steel. It starts off as this big blob of metal. When you're done, you're looking at this sword. There are days where I have to step back . . . it's really an incredible thing."

Similar to Jake Weidmann, the master penman, Kevin treats his role with a level of duty and gravity. He's a member of the American Bladesmith Society, which was founded in 1976 when bladesmiths were on the verge of becoming extinct in America. (The society now has almost 1,500 members.) Part of their tradition is the official ABS Master Smith test, which is standardized: First your blade has to cut a free-hanging piece of rope in one swipe, chop through two-by-fours, shave hair, and withstand being put into a vise and bent to ninety degrees without breaking.

Kevin's day-to-day work is still in shorter blades and hunting knives because the sword market is so specialized. He has to wait for someone to pay him to do the swords he really wants to work on and only does about four or five a year. When he is commissioned to make a sword, it's a much more involved process; "a labor of love," he calls it. Kevin talks about how people ask to be buried with the swords he made, and one day, maybe a thousand years from now, someone will find his swords and the process will repeat again. He will find himself on the other side of that long line of tradition.

TRADITION GUIDES ALL craftsmen, but it also plays a role in who we all are as people. It contributes to our sense of identity, our personal lives, and our family bonds. My mother's side of our family is Polish, only a couple of generations off the boat. Something I remember vividly from childhood—and that continues to this day—is sharing *oplatek* before Christmas Eve dinner, a tradition from the old country that goes back to the Middle Ages. The ritual centers around a thin rectangular wafer, usually with a nativity scene imprinted on it. Each person breaks off a small piece of the wafer and shares it with someone else, along with well wishes and a hug and kiss. It's a simple thing, but because I can remember sharing the wafer with all my relatives, past and present, it looms large in my memory. It's an example of why traditions are so powerful—they tie us to loved ones who are no longer with us. We can speak to them through the memory of the tradition, and through our continued engagement with that tradition. It also ties me to all the different versions of myself through the years: I remember partaking in the ritual as a boy, as a young man, as an adult, as a father. Traditions center us, give us a sense of home when we're there and, when we've left, a connection back to that home—even if by then it only exists in our hearts.

I went to Catholic school throughout my childhood and to mass every weekend with my family. As an altar boy, I knew the service inside and out and was as fluent in its details as with my favorite TV shows and action figures. By the time I was an adult, I felt like I didn't need church anymore, or maybe that I had had enough of it for one lifetime. But like many of the lapsed, I missed it: The longer it was absent from my life, the more I found myself pining for that place to go to, that connection to my past. There was a hole in my life.

When I eventually returned to church, it was nondenominational and not at all like the Catholic services I remembered. It was a nice enough experience, but it didn't feel like church, or rather, not what I thought of as church. The rituals and objects and clothing and processes and moments that I had long associated with church and Catholic mass were absent. It hit me how tightly those traditions were tied to who I am. About three years ago I returned to the Catholic Church and took renewed comfort in the traditions behind the Mass, the ceremony, the vestments, and the rituals. In some ways, I'm still searching for that feeling—of doing something that you know so well, so automatically, that it feels like home.

We're seeking tradition to create meaning.
—GERI LITTLEJOHN, *musician and flutemaker*

I MET GERI Littlejohn at her studio in a beautiful stretch outside of Asheville, North Carolina, at a spot where the green hills rise and drop down and rise again, a marvel of nature's geometric beauty. The sky stretches out for miles and, at certain times of day, it reflects colors you've never seen before up there—as though God were doing some painting. The drive in is enough to make you want to move there and never look back.

Thirty years ago, as an undergraduate student at Duke University, Geri met renowned Native American flutemaker

Hawk Littlejohn. After attending some Native American ceremonies, including her first sweat lodge, she found herself
magnetically drawn to the customs and the rituals she found
there. Those early experiences gave her a sense of meaning
and belonging. In a barter with Hawk for one of his handmade flutes, she agreed to work for him part-time. It was an
informal apprenticeship, with Geri sanding and drilling holes
in the flutes, observing the process, and learning about the
role of music in Native American ceremony. After graduation
Geri began to work for Hawk full-time, learning the practice
of making the instruments, along with the tradition in which
Hawk, a Cherokee, was deeply embedded. She fell in love with
all of it, including Hawk himself, and the two got married.

Geri was not born Native American, but her own childhood was shaped by a strong connection to the natural world.
She spent her summers outdoors on her grandparents' ten-
acre farm in Maine. With each passing year, communing
with the same piece of land, the same trees, the same lake,
she began to feel all its aliveness. She felt like she *knew*
it all. When she met Hawk in college and experienced the
Cherokee way of life, its interdependence with and reverence
for nature made intuitive sense to her. "That's where all the
wisdom traditionally came from among native people," Geri
told me. "The land is the teacher."

Nature was the binding force in Geri and Hawk's lives
and their work. The flutes came from the Earth—bamboo
and wood and fire—and they provided healing, communicated with spirits, and united the community. Geri became
a flute player as well, something that Hawk regularly

encouraged before he passed away in 2000. After he died, Geri made it her mission to spread his craft, music, and wisdom wherever she could. Eighteen years later, her life is still intimately wrapped up with the flutes and the music.

TO MAKE HER flutes, Geri casts a wide net, using materials native to the area—whether that's bamboo she harvests on her land, branches she finds nearby, or sentimental pieces of wood that people bring to her. From Geri I learned how the diameter of the bamboo is proportional to the sound's depth of pitch—the wider, the lower. How properly spacing the air holes creates the pentatonic scale in music. How the air from the breath moves through the distinctive two ducts on the Native American flute (which I had thought was just hollow all the way through).

Geri sees the flute as a living entity, with desires of its own that it can communicate directly. She sends the instruments—like companions—to accompany the sick, and she becomes attached to them in a way that could only happen with a living thing. I love what I do, but when I finish a bike and release it out into the world, I am ready to let it go. I no longer consider it mine.

Geri's connection goes a step further. She develops a genuine and lasting relationship with her instruments. There are particular flutes she becomes so close with during the creation process that she tells their new owners that if they ever tire of them to please send them back to her. The thought of the flute being unwanted and unplayed, buried in the back of the closet, is too much for her.

There's something egalitarian about the Native American flute, especially in the way Geri talked about it. When I told her that I had no idea how to play, she said that as long as I knew how to breathe and tap my fingers that I could do it. I hadn't thought about it so elementally like that: the breath—our life force—going through the flute and coming out the other end as music.

Despite her decades of experience, Geri didn't care for a label like "master craftsman," and I don't think it was just humility. Looking at flutemaking as a whole, on a long enough timeline, she still considers herself a learner. Understanding her purpose also makes her uninterested in the levels of distinction that create barriers between new-comers and experts. The simplicity and availability of the instrument are the point. *If you can breathe, you can play.*

The Native American flute "opens up this avenue of music for people who had it shut," she told me, and she was once one of those people. Geri has never been able to read music. As a high schooler playing clarinet, she played only by ear, something teachers told her was not the "proper" way. That exclusion bothered her in that it seemed to cut off that world, and she eventually lost interest. When she rediscovered music through Hawk and the wooden flute, she came at it from the direction that made sense to her: intuitively. It became about feeling, not knowing. Now she keeps the door open wide enough that anyone who is interested can step through.

Something that distinguished Geri from the other craftsmen I've met is she seemed less focused on exact measurements. There was something improvisatory and instinct-based, even *feel*-based, about the whole creation process. She continually reiterated the need to give the bamboo our "time and loving energy" and that making the flutes was not about imposing our will on the material but transforming it—with its agreement and help. We were engaged in a reciprocal relationship with the instrument.

Even the tools we used—the small propane torches, the screwdrivers heated to make the air holes, the saws—weren't specialized in any way. After the episode aired, a viewer contacted me, wanting to know specific diameter and length measurements so he could make a flute at home. I couldn't even tell him. I said Geri didn't seem too concerned about those things, so he shouldn't be either. It was more about creation and our connectedness to the material and the final object.

It reminded me of those cultural artifacts in which imperfection is an intentional quality, like the Navajo rugs or the Japanese *wabi-sabi*. (Geri actually lived in Japan for a large chunk of her childhood, so perhaps this rubbed off on her.) Hawk used to say: "Keep ego out of the way and become a hollow bone."

For Geri, her craft is a hollow bone, a means to an end. It is a way to partake in a rich tradition.

Traditions are particularly present in the daily lives of many Native Americans, and it's interesting to consider this through the lens of someone like Geri, who was not born into the culture; she adopted it by choice. Coming from the outside offers a new perspective: on the purpose of traditions,

how they operate, how they create structure and bring con-
nectivity to our lives.

She has raised her son in the Native American tradition and has been a participant in it for more than half her
life, so her origin seems beside the point. This is what she
has become. And as a flutemaker and player, she occupies
a central role in her adopted tradition. Songs are for social
gatherings, ceremony, prayers, healing, grieving, celebrating,
and daily activities from grinding the corn to weaving. The
ceremonial songs are about continuity, whether that's the
fire-lighting song or the song that greets the day.

"Some of the songs help to cultivate a relationship with
the natural world," Geri said, "in a language that's not necessarily human. And as humans you need help from the universe." In Native American tradition there is no separation
between the individual and the world, or the physical and
the spiritual. They are all one and the same.

The key to ritual is the repetition. Once we sing a song
or recite a prayer so many times that we know it so well, we
"reach the next level of being the prayer," as Geri put it. We
join all those who are singing with us and those who have
sung this song in the past and those who will sing it in the
future. We cross time and space and inhabit the song and
reach a place where the ritual is doing us.

Geri confessed that when she was young, like a lot of
young people, she embraced rebellion and change. But
that approach gave way to the opposite in her adulthood: a
respect for how things are done, a belief that those things
that last have lasted for a reason. Her way of showing

gratitude to those who made sacrifices in the past is by not changing it.

It's about trust and faith: *This way works*. She and I spoke about how this idea is echoed in working with our hands. Whether it's bamboo flutes or motorcycles, people discovered some time ago that this was the best way to do it. That's the legacy they left. It doesn't mean you don't modify or improvise, but you need to know what it is first before you can do that.

I never met Hawk Littlejohn, but it seems clear that he touched so many lives. And Geri continues to do the same, in her own way. The spiritual connection Geri has to her instrument—even during the process of its becoming that instrument—is profound. It's all intertwined: her craft, the music, the Native American tradition, and her late husband's memory. "I hope that there are always native people still measuring cane and wood by their hands and sticks," Hawk once said, "and pass those sticks and the size of their hands down so we don't lose the voice of the people, the ancient songs . . . all that is in the flute."

ALL THE CRAFTSMEN I visit on the show are tied up in a rich and fascinating tradition that flows through all of their work. When I asked cooper Jim Gaster to describe what he did for a living, he said he works with dead crafts and brings them back to life. A goldsmith named Susan McDonough follows a process first used 3,500 years ago. Puppet maker Tim Selberg feels connected to the roots of vaudeville, which is a part of American history that has died out. Ben Heinemann makes duck decoys, a tradition that reaches back over a thousand years.

As much as things change and progress is made, there is this thread that runs through and connects all of it. We are building off a solid tradition that connects people whom we have never met but who are part of our ancestral line. It's the reason a craftsman is never really doing something alone. If we think of ourselves as part of this long continuum, no one is ever actually starting from scratch.

13: SHRINKING THE WORLD

A few months after my panic attacks first began to colonize my life, they rose up to take over completely. One spring morning in 1999, I was driving on the expressway to a meeting for Xerox when, all of a sudden, I had a hard time breathing. There was this intense constricted feeling in my chest and the pain just got tighter and tighter, like a hand gripping my chest and squeezing. Then my heart started pounding rapidly and wouldn't stop. A month or so after my attacks in Texas, a doctor taught me some breathing exercises, so my instinct was to try those. But they just made me hyperventilate. I was terrified: I pulled off at an exit, grabbed my cell phone, and called 911.

"Nine-one-one, what's your emergency?" a voice said.

"I think I'm having a heart attack," I said, pushing the sounds through shortened breath. Just saying the words sent my mind into a tailspin.

"Where are you? Can you pull over?"

I turned into the parking lot of a Mobil gas station.

"Just did."

"Okay, stay there," she said. "Paramedics are on their way."

When EMS arrived in an ambulance, two people popped out and rushed the car. I opened my driver's side door and they checked my heart and ran a series of tests. One of the paramedics let me know that my heart seemed fine.

"What's been going on with your life?" she said, a bit more calmly. "Why do you think this might've happened?"

I told her about the scuba dive, the Texas trip, the nervousness that had become a semi-regular part of my life.

"You're not having a heart attack," she said. "I think you're just having a panic attack." *Just* a panic attack. It didn't do much to put me at ease. They loaded me onto a stretcher and put me into the back of the ambulance. As we rode to the hospital, I still couldn't settle. I ripped the oxygen mask off my face and was tugging at some of the wires. "Leave those," the paramedic in the back told me. "We're almost there."

At the hospital I was still so agitated, moving around and pulling at everything, that they had to sedate me. A few hours later I woke up to an IV in my arm, the steady beeping of a sterile white room, and the late afternoon light slicing through the blinds.

For two days I was kept for evaluation; tests on my heart determined there was nothing medically wrong with me. It was like I had brought it on myself. I had basically *thought* myself into the hospital, which was hard for me to wrap my head around. Everything about those days is blurry because I was on sedatives for most of the time.

When I was released, the reality hit like a harsh and brutal light: I couldn't go back to work. I was too consumed with fear to do anything. Afraid to leave the house and be caught in an attack in a crowded place far from home. Afraid to drive anywhere or even ride my motorcycle, because an episode on the road would kill me. Afraid that my brain had the power to cause so much damage. I was put on a series of drugs for anxiety, which reached such high doses that I couldn't function. Walking properly became an issue, and it took me half a day just to cut the lawn. Even holding a conversation was difficult—not that I wanted to.

After talking with the doctors at the hospital, and in follow-ups during my recovery, my mind started to connect the dots. It dawned on me that what I was going through wasn't new at all. It was a condition I'd had when I was young but never really named or sought help for. I had almost blocked it out.

As a kid I was often filled with a nervous energy and discomfort, anxiety about upcoming events, places I had to go, and being away from home. I was a shy kid who just wanted to be liked. I was too afraid to meet people, or introduce myself, and it took me a while to open up even once I got to know someone. Neither of my parents had any idea what to do about it or if anything could be done.

One of my earliest memories of it being an issue was at the start of second grade. The school had changed my homeroom from the year before, along with the teacher I really liked. After I heard this, I flipped out; I wouldn't get on the bus and I started screaming, throwing a tantrum and running around the kitchen table. My dad had to come home from work and he walked in the door decidedly unhappy. All six feet and four inches of him grabbed me and carried me under his arm, horizontal like a stack of wood, and put me in his truck to take me to school. After a few weeks of my shenanigans, the school shifted me back to the old homeroom.

Not too long after this, I signed up for Cub Scout camp, something I was incredibly excited about. But once I got there, I couldn't stop crying. I was homesick and miserable, especially around four p.m. when my mom usually got home from work. The counselors let me call her, and after a couple of days I was fine, loving it enough to join the Scouts year round.

Being in the Scouts was an eye-opening experience for me. I loved the creation aspect: turning empty ice cream tubs into knights' helms by wrapping them in tinfoil and cutting out a visor, making suede pouches with lace and handles, carving race cars for the pinewood derby. Near Detroit, the pinewood derby is no joke because so many of the parents work for the major car companies. Some other kids' cars were wind tested, slick painted, and weight shifted, so I got destroyed, but I still loved it. I took the Scouts seriously and responded to every aspect of it: the learning, the projects, the outdoors, the uniform, the badges. I wanted nothing else than to become a Boy Scout and used to pore over the handbook, learning anything I could. I wanted to camp—living in a tent for the weekends and exploring outside, making fires and carving wood sticks, was what I dreamed of. But my separation anxiety was too intense for the camping trip. It tore me up, but my anxiety put up a wall, and I absolutely couldn't climb over it. So I quit.

Now in my late twenties, it had all come roaring back, in a biological form, a physical manifestation of all that anxiety. It was as though it had been laying low, building up mass and speed, and getting stronger. And then it struck, in effect turning me into an agoraphobic. The world became a scary place where the littlest thing could cause an attack. Whether one came on or not was beside the point; I was ruled by them, because the fear of getting trapped in one was all I thought about.

My world collapsed around me, shrinking to a size I could barely handle. The attacks could be set off by a sound, a smell, maybe a feeling. The biggest fear was an anxiety attack that was big enough for other people to recognize. It's the kind of condition that feeds on itself, a snake eating its tail. While I was beginning to go through it, I'd have anxiety about the fact that I was going through it, that people would laugh or point at me, which would explode it into something exponentially worse.

Other times I would create alternate worlds, a series of what-ifs that would spin out of control and—before I knew it—I had thought myself into an attack. Every location where I had an attack became a trigger: the drugstore, the movie theater, the grocery store, this parking lot, that street. There was no safety anywhere except home, and not really even there; but there was no alternative. At Xerox I went on disability and essentially locked myself in my house.

Hardly anyone knew I was suffering. I was too afraid of being perceived as a failure or as a weak person, an issue that lasted for a very long time. There was an element of false masculinity at work too. *I'm a tough guy*, I thought, and these episodes—and the fear that came with them—didn't fit with how I saw myself. They didn't mesh with how I wanted the world to view me. I've also long been fairly superstitious and was afraid to talk about them because I thought even the words would launch an attack. Like I'd conjure one to life through speech.

My solution up to then for any problem in my life was taking control. I thought of that as my skill set. But the panic disorder, by its very nature, resisted any kind of control. I bought every single book I could find on panic, anxiety, depression, and started poring through them all. But my trying to wrest control made things worse. I would read about all the other symptoms that I'd yet to have but could look forward to. *Did I have that too? Was I going to?* The one thing I knew how to do was backfiring. So my trust in the world, and my confidence in myself, was shattered.

THE ONE THING that seemed to get my mind off the fear and the anxiety was working in my garage. I had my motorcycle in there, along with my brother's bike, which needed some work. My home garage was immaculate, and hours could pass in that workshop without a thought about the panic attacks. It was heated and comfortable—even in the cold—with oriented strand board (like particleboard) on the walls, so everything was easy to attach. There were outlets every four feet on each wall and lights in banks of three on the ceiling, so it was very bright. The floor was epoxied and the workbenches were built rugged enough to hold the weight of a dozen engines.

That garage was a savior: It allowed me an escape and a release during a time when I was petrified that I'd get struck by lightning again. Afraid of what the world was doing to my body, I turned inward to the one thing I felt I could handle: working on motorcycles. The garage became my sanctuary. Working with my hands gave me a singular focus, with no room for anxiety to sneak in. It was all in front of me: *This piece connects to this piece.* I had the final say of when to stop and when to move on, which helped me regain the control I had lost in the world outside of my garage.

The more I worked on the bikes, the comfort gave way to the challenge, to the deep well of knowledge that I wanted to explore. Metal, torches, and welding had long held a fascination for me, and motorcycles had been part of my life since I was eight years old. I started to reclaim the territory of my mind, my body, and my life. I would no longer be a passenger. Those months were the worst experience of my life and the best thing that ever happened to me. They laid the groundwork for the new self that would emerge.

I DISTINCTLY REMEMBER the day I saw color for the first time. Color as it was meant to be seen. It was a Sunday morning and I was lying in bed staring at a piece of stained glass that was hanging in the window. It was an abstract thing I'd made in community college, something I'd looked at a million times without thinking much about it. But for some reason, that morning, I finally *saw* it: the fieriness of the orange, the warmth of the red like heat I could feel on my skin, the brightness and vibrancy of the greens and blues. At the time I thought I was hallucinating, but quickly enough the fear and noise started to settle. I realized how beautiful it was, how sharp all the colors were coming through. Like a gradient screen had been removed from my eyes.

There was so much more going on around me than I had realized. It was like I hadn't had the time for it, or the right eyes to see it, or the courage to look. During the months of panic attacks, the world had been shrinking bit by bit for me, and I thought that shrinking would protect me.

But that morning, for the first time in a long time, the world *expanded*. I realized how strong my mind was, how it could brighten or lessen, accept or ignore, amplify or quiet. I saw what was worth valuing—how I could steer my life into those things that mattered to me—and I wanted more of it.

14: LEGACY

The great use of life is to spend it for something that will outlast it. —WILLIAM JAMES

To be a craftsman is to be a time capsuler, a creator of permanence. The object and the skills behind it are a form of immortality, like April Wagner told me about her blown-glass pieces. "They will outlive me," she said, "and they will tell future generations something about me." I couldn't agree more.

It was not too long ago that what you did was such a part of you—your identity and your world—that it was your family name: Smith, Cooper, Sawyer, Mason. Future generations would carry on that skill, and that's how it—and you—got carried through time. There was pride and honor in sending it forward. It was a reminder that life isn't just about us—it's about what remains when we're gone. Our legacy.

I wanted the word "legacy" in the television show's title and I guide just about every interview to this topic because I feel it's at the crux of what craftsmen do and who we are. We learn and receive, we internalize and utilize, we teach and we pass on. Some craftsmen understand this intuitively. There's an optimism about the work, a belief that what we're doing will outlast us.

My goal with the show is to embrace things that last. Things we can hold. Things we can learn from. Things that tell a story or give us an opportunity to celebrate people who came before us. Things that can tell future people something about us. The objects I make on the show, in other people's shops, flawed as they may be, are intimate things. They carry my personal touch, the influence of the craftsman who taught me, the tradition behind the object, and the legacy that's being passed down in the process. They are packed with so much.

Bryan Galloup, a guitar maker I met in the first season of *A Craftsman's Legacy*, teaches at a school connected to his shop where his students live. After they graduate, he sends them out into the world to share the craft. "The compliment is when employers call you [and say] 'These people are ready,'" he told me, "or you watch them break away on their own." The success of Bryan's students becomes a key part of his legacy. It's like how Tibetan Buddhists say that if the student isn't better than the teacher, then the teacher has failed. Bryan described his legacy as having "long arms," and that is the perfect image: *long arms*. It suggests reaching out, which is what a legacy is when you get down to it.

It's not a passive thing, like what is accidentally left behind. It's what you *choose* to share with the future. There's intention behind it, and that intention matters.

In the second season of *A Craftsman's Legacy*, I met Curtis Buchanan, who wanted his legacy to be something so simple and poignant: the amount and quality of the time he spent with his children. He wanted to pack their lunches and see them off to school, do all the little things that eventually comprise an entire childhood. So he quit his job and began working with wood out of his Tennessee home. He had a base of knowledge from his Depression-era parents, who, when they wanted something, just made it.

Curtis built a shop at home so his daughters could see where he works, what he does, and what a woodshop smells like. While doing carpentry work, he met Dave Sawyer, one of the few people making Windsor chairs in the country. Named after the town of England where they were first made at the start of the eighteenth century, Windsor chairs are defined as a chair in which all the parts meet at the seat. Sawyer is such a legend in the trade that his work is in museums. He took Curtis on, sharing the knowledge of this specific and beloved corner of furniture-making. Thirty years later, Curtis has become so accomplished that his Windsor chairs are now in the Tennessee governor's mansion as well as Thomas Jefferson's Virginia home, Monticello. But you wouldn't know about any of this success just from meeting him. What seemed to matter the most to him was how he was impacting those he loved.

If you really want to learn how to do something with your hands . . . then along with that responsibility comes the fact that you have to teach other people. Or else you're not doing anything for the craft. You're killing it.
—NOEL GRAYSON, *bow and arrow maker*

ONE OF THE most satisfying experiences I've had shooting *A Craftsman's Legacy* was with Noel Grayson, a bow and arrow maker of Cherokee lineage who lives in Oklahoma. Noel has a long braided ponytail, graying sideburns, and deep, dark eyes. Noel has been honored as a Cherokee National Treasure, an award given only to a select few who exemplify the spirit of Cherokee crafts. We met at the Cherokee Heritage Center, which is both a community gathering place and a living museum. Noel works in the Diligwa section (the word literally means "the open place where the grass grows"), a hunting village designed to reflect the Native American life of the 1700s, when trade with Europeans was just beginning.

For visitors and tours, Noel does demonstrations and teaches classes on flint knapping (making stone tools), tanning hides, and making moccasins and baskets, as well as the ancient technique of twining, lacing strands together from natural materials. But his favorite things to make, just like when he was a kid, are still bows and arrows. He and his brothers used to make and play with them, and though they grew out of it, he never did. He said the process still "makes me feel like a kid." I feel like this is a common theme with craftsmen; we're all tapping into that childlike sense of creation and wonder.

ARCHEOLOGISTS HAVE RECENTLY found evidence in Africa indicating bows and arrows may have been invented over seventy thousand years ago, far earlier than previously thought. If this is proven to be true, it would represent a gigantic leap forward in prehistoric man's toolmaking ability. The devices eventually spread all over the world, and around 2500 B.C., the Central Asians invented a smaller and shorter bow, which was more useful on horseback. Native Americans in North America invented their own bows and arrows relatively late, around 500 A.D., as a more lethal and accurate weapon than the spears they had been using.

Long after the introduction of firearms around the fourteenth century, Native American tribes continued to use bows and arrows for hunting, fighting, even fishing. One advantage is that bows and arrows can be made conveniently, out of what's lying around. Plus, they make hunting and attacking far more quiet than they would be with a booming gun. Though, of course, the bow and arrow requires enormous skill to use quickly and efficiently. The weapon has long been associated with Native Americans—in history, in legend, and in art. Noel learned the craft from his father and other elders in the manner that indigenous people have been using for thousands of years: through the oral tradition.

Long after the written word and then the printing press gave Europeans a more permanent way to record their knowledge, history, and stories, the Native Americans still had to rely on the spoken word. Without access to books (or to a formal education that fostered literacy*), the Native American tribes passed their culture on from person to person, group to group, generation to generation. In addition, because white settlers were constantly moving or wiping out tribes, there had to be less reliance on anything marked down. Native Americans had to trust their heads and hearts more than any physical record.

Because of this, the tribes' survival depended on those who carried on important information, tribe history, and collective traditions. It's one of the reasons that the elders of Native Americans are treated with such reverence—they are the libraries and the schools and the storytellers of whole tribes. When they die, entire worlds are lost. Even in the modern world, where recording devices are literally in everyone's pocket, the oral tradition is still an integral element of Native American society.

As Noel was showing us around the Heritage Center, the crew and I were scouring for places to shoot the episode. Noel took me into the winter council house, which was a large hut-style building with a dirt floor, a fire pit in the center, and an open-domed top for the smoke to clear. Sectioned into equal areas for each tribe, it was where the high council, the leaders for each tribe, would meet to discuss affairs.

---

* Even after Native Americans were brought—and forced—into the fold of formal schooling, they were taught European customs, not their own. It was about assimilation, first and foremost, not necessarily education.

Once I stepped in, I immediately responded to the raw openness. With nowhere to hide or be alone, the council house was designed to foster a community, in the best sense of the word. It was a physical reminder that each individual relied on everyone else. A cold front had moved in that day, and as the cool air chilled our breath and rain dropped through the vent hole in the ceiling, I knew this ambience would come through on screen. I couldn't imagine a better place to shoot not just the interview, but the whole episode.

Once we set up to shoot and got the fire got going, the brisk air warmed up quickly. There was no visual distraction, nothing in the background, just a crackling fire and the deep, sonorous sound of Noel's voice. The plan was to make an arrow through the ancient process of flint knapping, so we sat down on a couple of deer pelts in front of all the tools we needed: sticks, rocks, plant stalks, feathers, and the fire.

Flint knapping, the process of making stone tools, is about four million years old. The method uses only naturally occurring materials; not a single mechanical tool—and I use "mechanical" in the most basic way imaginable—is used. The resourcefulness reflects how Native tribes survived. Though they traded, they mostly relied on the materials that were local to their home. It was a life of constant adaptation. As such, there are no standardized materials for Native American bows and arrows. A bow and arrow in Arizona will look different from one in Oklahoma, because it has to. The specific resources and deprivations in each area determined what they could make.

For our arrows, Noel and I started with a piece of river cane, which is similar to bamboo. We rubbed it against a rough spot of flat rock to sand the nodes down, a practice which the people spent all their free time doing because, as Noel said, "we constantly used them." I was struck by how Noel frequently used the word "we" when discussing his Cherokee ancestors. It was an enormously revealing language choice. The tribe is a collective united through time and Noel naturally considers them all one. I'm close with my family and connected to my heritage, but I never once would say, *We came here from Poland*. It wouldn't even occur to me to do so.

The next step was to heat up our cane over the fire to get it malleable. Then we pressed it down to straighten it, and it moved far more easily than I thought it would. Throughout the process, we did not use a single measuring device but our own bodies: We relied only on feel and the eye test, holding the cane up like you would hold up a rifle to get a look down the barrel.

Using antler bone, we next knocked off a thin and sharp piece of rock, a flake, and that became our knife. With that knife we sliced the turkey feather that we would put on the back of the arrow as fletching. We then snapped a stalk of dogbane plant and pulled a thin fiber off it to use as thread to tie the feather on the back of the arrow, which would stabilize it in flight. Afterward we knocked that same sharp rock into a smaller flake, which would become our arrow point. Once it was the right size and shape, we tied the arrowhead on using plant fiber and then heated pinesap by the fire to make the glue to bind it in place. The entire process is a model of efficiency and self-sufficiency, something Native Americans had to master, especially after European settlers forced them out of their original homeland.

As someone fascinated with tools, machines, and technology, it was eye-opening to use only primitive tools. I loved the challenge and how it forced me to think about the craft process differently. Noel and I didn't even have a knife, which I think of as so basic that I don't go anywhere without one. Throughout my time at the Heritage Center, I felt so connected to the land, what it has to offer, and what our responsibility to it should be. All Native American tribes share an understanding that their own health is ultimately wrapped up in the Earth's health.

Like with Geri Littlejohn, it was clear while Noel and I made our arrows that there were two levels to what we were doing: the work and the larger context, the culture behind the work. Inside the council house I was engaged in this primal experience, the sense that we were digging down to the origin, to the source of things. In the darkness, my body on the deer pelt, Noel quietly tossing the occasional branch onto the fire, my mind entered a calm and altered state. But as a visitor, it was also important that I pay respect to the cultural aspect and not just take what I needed and leave. There were larger implications to what I was doing, and I was sensitive to the long history of violence and exploitation that hangs over the treatment of Native Americans in this country.

Getting to shoot that arrow afterward, this item that we built from the Earth, was the perfect final moment. I'd always been really into target shooting, even practicing a few times a week at an indoor range with a compound bow, which is easier to use because its mechanical pulley shape reduces the load on the shooter. With Noel that day, as I drew back the bow and struggled with the pull weight, trembling a little, it was difficult for me to aim. Noel's approach was completely different. He studied the target for a moment and then, in one fluid motion, drew the bow and released, faster than I'd ever seen someone do it.

Noel is a gentle soul who clearly loved showing people traditional skills. Even though he's taught flint knapping thousands of times, he still feels this jolt from someone figuring it out. He got this little encouraging smile every time I did something right. It was clear he believed his purpose was to act as a conduit or pathway. His legacy mattered to him, and I thought again of the idea of the "hollow bone": open, willing to be filled, a channel for things to pass through. It's a shame that some of those things have been lost—and not through time and neglect, but through willful destruction.

Legacy is something that many craftsmen understand, but when considering Native American culture, or any culture that has been under constant threat, this aspect takes on a particular urgency. There is genuine fear that the skills and the culture can vanish to history. In 1500 there were millions* of Native Americans in what Europeans called the New World. By 1900 it was down to around two hundred thousand.

---

* Estimates range from two to eighteen million.

For some people, a legacy is a physical thing, literally what they leave behind. Nathan Bower's children may keep their father's skeleton clocks in their future homes and point them out to explain what their father once did. April Wagner's glass sculptures may end up in houses far from her studio and illuminate some room or move someone she has never met. After the craftsmen are gone, their objects carry their story. For others, the legacy is more abstract: It's the knowledge or philosophical message they share with those who care enough to carry it on.

Because many of the craftsmen we feature on the show are or were once teachers, when I work with them, that experience always comes through in their manner and approach. They are more natural about breaking down the steps and leading me through them. I notice how they don't treat their own common sense as someone else's, which is a mistake that plenty of experts make. A natural teacher can empathize with, even inhabit, the mind of a beginner.

Off and on for some years, I taught motorcycle-based metal shaping classes, which I've always enjoyed because the students are like sponges, ready to learn. I'm a big proponent of the idea that knowledge comes from errors. Skill is not so much knowing how to create something; it's knowing how to fix the problems that arise during the process of creation. It comes down to a simple equation: The more mistakes you make, the more you know how to correct, the more you learn.

I love working with people of various skill levels, because the interaction always yields some new lesson or point of view. Recently, my daughter and I built a bird feeder together. The bottom base of it was a formed piece of copper, which is basically the beginning of a bowl, one of the first shapes you learn in metal classes. We measured the size and cut out the copper, which was too thick and rigid to bend with our bare hands. But after we heated it up and then quenched it in cold water it came out buttery soft, easy for us to form. Because this is something I've done for decades, I take it for granted, but my daughter's eyes just popped. "That's crazy!" she said, marveling at the change before her eyes. Seeing it new like that was like falling in love all over again.

I used to teach metal shaping on a step-by-step basis, which is a typical method used by instructors. Most of the time you will pack as many projects and shapes as possible in a few days so students can bring trinkets home with them. Over time I began to feel like maybe they were sacrificing the knowledge in exchange for the souvenirs. If I called my students up and asked them to replicate the simplest project, would they be able to? Were they retaining the knowledge? Did they ever really have it? Or had they just been following steps?

Steps are useful until a problem arises. Then you have no idea what to do. Do you go back? Go forward? And there's no objective way to know if you're ready to advance. If you don't understand it, then you're just learning instructions. For something as dynamic as metal shaping you need to be able to adjust your approach as the shape is being developed. If you make a mistake, you need to know how to correct it. Actually, you need to be able to recognize that it was a mistake in the first place.

I took a break from teaching workshops because of other commitments, but when I got back to it I scrapped the idea of designing the class around projects and instead built it around fundamentals. I stopped aiming to send students home with physical objects and focused on sending them off with basic skills. These were less visible but more valuable. When they got back to their lives, if they chose to, they could extend their knowledge.

For instance, on day one we spent the entire day making bowls. It's a basic shape but also the building block for 90 percent of metal work. First we did it in mild steel, then in aluminum, because I wanted them to have that tangible memory of the difference. They remember that one took half the day and the other took thirty minutes. We also worked on the easiest way to fix problems that inevitably arise, and it often involves taking a hammer to it. I feel like part of my legacy, besides instilling the basic skills, is helping the students to think for themselves and accumulate experience, and offering a peek at something that might light a fire for them.

The word "legacy" can mean something different to everyone. The idea is that it came from us, but it exists outside ourselves, and it's there after we're gone. Brass horn maker Richard Seraphinof told me that the most important element of his legacy is his students—more than any music he plays or horn he makes. Just like April Wagner called her pieces her children, puppet maker Tim Selberg called his "little pieces of immortality."

Fly rod makers Jeff Wagner and Casimira Orlowski have been teaching cane rod building for over twenty years and can't imagine stopping anytime soon. "At the end you've done a lot more than made a rod, sold a rod," Jeff told me, "you've made friends with somebody . . . We've met people through this all over the world."

Noel Grayson told me that teaching children is an especially important part of his work. The secret he tells kids and adults alike: "If you make them for the love of doing it, then you'll make good ones." Of course, the skills he offers are important, but transmitting his love for the craft is just as significant a part of his legacy. What I learned from Noel and from so many of the craftsmen I've met is that we need to start valuing our legacy while we're alive, because we still have time to adapt it, make something of it. What do we want it to be? The legacy is not just what we made, or even what we taught, but the lives we touched.

15: INDIVIDUALITY

Look for the person in the object.
—JAMES KRENOV, *woodworker and author*

In some capacity, most craftsmen, myself included, see themselves as going against the flow of mainstream society. Or possibly we feel separate from the flow entirely, in a different stream altogether. Making an independent living with your hands involves marching to your own beat and being comfortable with the sound. It means going down untrodden paths and being okay if there is not a soul around for miles in any direction. It's heading out there without knowing where you might end up and laying claim to your own piece of land. It's about individuality, which is the soul of innovation.

One of my favorite aspects of *A Craftsman's Legacy* is meeting and learning about all kinds of people. Not just what they make and how, but why they got into their craft. What's their origin story? What motivated them to start? What continues to drive them? What inspires and influences them in their work and life? No one chooses to shape their whole lives around an object and an act unless they have some passion and emotional connection to it.

Each craftsman has a unique story, but one common theme that sticks out is this: It's intentional. Often they are on one path, feeling and fumbling around as we all do, until they reach a eureka moment: *This is it. This is what I want to do. This is what I was* meant *to do.* It's a spiritual realization. Hearing those accounts sometimes gives me chills.

THERE'S AN OLD saying, and though I'm not sure how accurate it is, I think it's revealing: *Artists sign their name where you can see it; craftsmen sign their name where you can't.* Art brings attention to itself; its purpose is to stand out, stop people in their tracks, get them to think or feel—for better or for worse.

Craftsmanship can do that too—like April Wagner's desire for people to connect emotionally to her glass pieces—but often it sits more quietly and unassumingly. It's more interested in fitting perfectly where it needs to be than in taking center stage. It's unfortunate that most of the time craftsmanship gets noticed when it's bad craftsmanship, when there's a problem. It often comes down to a question of utilitarian value. Can the item be used for something? I think maybe it's less explicitly celebrated than art because it has that set purpose, which comes with predetermined expectations.

Even though craftsmen and their work have been taken for granted, the word itself has never been more popular. Craftsmanship has been hijacked by salesmen and co-opted by advertisers, who have watered it down through misuse. Similar words, like "artisan," "bespoke," and "handcrafted," are slapped onto all kinds of things that have nothing to do with craftsmanship. Every time a fast-food sandwich is called "handcrafted," the word dies a little bit more. Marketers understand that each consumer wants to feel special. After all, there's a uniformity in society, whether it's our furniture, our vacation spots, or our ambitions. Marketers play off our desire to be an individual—or at least, to feel like one. As a consequence, craftsmanship is losing its connotation of singularity.

The individuality sold to us through commercials is an illusion. Of course it benefits big-box stores and corporations if we all have the same taste and conception of beauty—then they only have to make so many varieties of things. Often when an original or eccentric product comes out, it's from the same parent company that makes the top seller. For example, the major beer brands have bought up most of the craft beer companies. So they're selling the mainstream and then they're selling the counterculture too.

True individuality is an uphill and constant battle. You have to fight to make things your own wherever you can. I used to think about this over the stove making breakfast every morning. My ex-girlfriend has three kids—and partly because of the busyness of her life, she tended to rush things. I understand where it came from, and I don't blame her, but it was a fact.

Whoever got up first made breakfast for the kids, which meant pancakes. Hers were always all over the place: misshapen or often undercooked. You could tell by looking at them that her mind was elsewhere and she was trying to get on to the next thing. When it was my turn to make pancakes, I didn't care how long it took; I wanted each and every one to be as perfect as I could make it. They weren't something complicated like a soufflé, but that didn't matter to me. I focused on the process and putting myself into it. I took it seriously. The adage *How we do anything is how we do everything* is a philosophy I subscribe to.

There's a Greek word, *meraki*, that I love. We don't really have an equivalent word in English. It means putting yourself into something—your passion, your ingenuity, the *you* in you. That kind of individuality is worth informing everything we do.

Someone can come in here and I'll know exactly what they need. They don't know what they need.
—ERIC YELSMA, *jeans maker*

ON A WALL in the warehouse studio of Detroit Denim Co., behind a plate of glass, hangs a framed pair of jeans. The jeans themselves are unassuming; they're not there as a model of great craftsmanship. The reason is that they're a symbol of one person's dream of striking out on his own. The jeans, the very first pair that Eric Yelsma made, are "pretty awful," he confessed to me. "People joke that if *they* had done that the first time, they would've quit." But Eric knew he was onto something.

After fifteen years in the corporate world of the chemical industry, Eric ran headfirst into fate: Record oil prices put him out of a job. Though it had been steady work, it was "soul crushing," he said, and hindsight makes him grateful it happened. Even at the time, Eric was philosophical about the experience. He knew he could only control how he reacted to losing his job, so that's what he focused on.

It took Eric a full year to figure out what he should do next, but a seed had been planted long ago. His mother was a home economics teacher who had taught him how to sew, and he grew up to be a jeans lover and collector, owning up to thirty-nine pairs at one point. They were something he had appreciated all his life, and, in his memorable phrasing, he had a "burning ember of denim."

The spark that finally sent him on his path was his favorite pair of jeans. Eric had grown so attached to these pants that for years he had been taking them to his tailor to rescue them from the brink. Eventually it reached a point where she felt there was nothing to be done and Eric had to let them go. Like with losing his job, Eric once again transformed this ending into a beginning. He excitedly asked his tailor to make a new custom pair, and he had some ideas. But though she knew how to alter jeans, she was sure she couldn't make a pair from scratch.

Eric is not an ease-his-way-in kind of guy. His impulse was to jump in headfirst. So he cashed in some retirement savings and started buying machines and gathering material. Clothing manufacturing had been steadily moving overseas since the 1970s, so Eric was able to buy some great old sewing machines, well-built works of art that were gathering dust. I saw one of the machines, named Rosie after the name scratched into it. It is one hundred years old, and Eric still uses it every day.

As long as the machines are given regular maintenance, they won't break down. However, since there's no one left who can fix them, Eric's on his own when and if they do. For material, he insists on only sourcing denim from America. Only 1 percent of jeans are actually made in the United States today, and Eric told me that there's only one mill in North Carolina that makes the kind of denim he uses. He's since had offers to acquire denim from cheaper places overseas but he has kept to this pledge.

As so many great start-up businesses do, Eric's began in his garage (which is where I also started). I've often wondered: *What is it about garages?* I think it's because adults are free to play in there. It's home, but it's not our house, so there's room for who you want to be, not necessarily who you are. It's both closed off and open, and it can be filled with whatever you want it to be filled with. It's a place where we can better handle mistakes and accidents and messes and folly. It's where we dream.

Once Eric accepted that a serious business needed a larger place, he searched for space in the heart of Detroit. He insisted on a downtown location because he wanted the soul, the feel, and the history of the area. "Everything our jeans are, is about what this city offers and has been," he told me. He wanted his jeans, this great American invention, to be made and tied to the history of this great American city. He found a warehouse space, and Detroit Denim Co. was born.

His first plan was to sell wholesale to cosmopolitan cities like Chicago or San Francisco, but he changed course when he started thinking about what he wanted his company to be. "Be" in a larger sense of the word, as in what identity did he want for his business? Eric realized that forming a direct relationship between product and customer would be a huge plus, especially in a market where the item is designed to fit the specificity of a person's body. So he decided to sell directly to people: Customers could even come in and get measured on the grounds. They would be free to watch the jeans being made, be able to come back to have them fixed, meet the people who were involved in their production. There was a face and place and a name—his customers would feel connected and taken care of. They wouldn't just be a line on a profit and loss statement.

Eric's goal was not simply to open a clothing company; he wanted to connect with the quality of the pants and the uniqueness of each customer. The jeans he sells are expensive, but you get what you pay for—Eric's jeans are beautiful pieces of craftsmanship. One pair will outlast five pairs of jeans off the rack.

The word "factory" implies replication, defined as "any place producing a uniform product, without concern for individuality." This is decidedly *not* what Eric does. He embraces the hands-on approach, which is "really just going back to where it used to be," as he said. We forget that clothes were once made specifically for one body. We've progressed away from that into these generic categories—men and women; small, medium, and large—that really tell us nothing. Eric's jeans look to restore the individuality to one of the quintessential American products.

Blue jeans are iconic, associated with youth and American culture. The epitome of 1950s cool was Marlon Brando or James Dean in theirs and a white T-shirt, but jeans actually began as work pants. They were a functional solution to a real-life problem. In the 1850s German immigrant Levi Strauss opened up a general store in San Francisco to serve the slew of forty-niners who had headed out West chasing gold. Over time, miners would come to him asking for new kinds of pants, because their wool ones were getting torn to shreds in the mines. Straus tried pants made from the canvas he had lying around, which didn't work at all. Then he tried a type of woven cotton (*de Nîmes*— "from Nîmes," which is in France) which was both durable and comfortable. The miners loved them, and Strauss started to make more. In 1873, Straus teamed up with a Reno tailor named Jacob Davis who wanted to patent his idea of using rivets on pants, and jeans were born.

A century and a half later, 96 percent of Americans own at least one pair of jeans, and 60 percent of those people wear a pair to work at least four days a week. North America accounts for 40 percent of worldwide sales, which is not surprising, since jeans are an American invention with an American association. But everyone else loves them as well: Over 1.2 billion pairs of denim jeans are sold in the world each year. Most women own an average of seven; six for men. Eric told me that in Europe and Asia, customers are more willing to pay extra for a nice pair of jeans than Americans are. He thinks American jeans have become "victims of the mall. Kind of like the McDonaldization of food, we've done that with our clothes."

There's a relationship you can develop with a piece of clothing. It might bind you to a memory, a person, a time in your life, an association, or an emotional connection. A pair of jeans is a canvas of memories: the holes, scratches, even stains give them their personality. You're "walking around with this scrapbook of what you've done, who you are," Eric told me. Your clothes say something about you; your jeans, which some of us wear most of the week (or all the time), might say the most. They make a statement about the wearer, something about how we see ourselves and how we want to be seen. From the fit, style, leg type (tapered or straight), amount of room, color—figuring out what your pair of jeans is can be seen as a process of discovery and self-discovery. There's also a confidence that comes from wearing something that fits well. That fits only you. A good pair of jeans offers self-assuredness, a feeling that no one is occupying the spot that you're standing on. That no one possibly could.

There's great intention behind what Eric is doing with his business. He wrote a manifesto for the company that solidifies the culture, the type of people, the values, and the attention to the work that Detroit Denim Co. embodies. Among the maxims: *Run our business how we run our lives* and *Do things with purpose.*

Eric's jeans are selvedge (a merging of the term "self-edged"), which means the denim is woven on an older mechanical loom in a way that makes it sturdier, less likely to unravel, and more visually distinct. This higher quality denim represents only 1 percent of the jeans on the market. The jeans do cost more, but they're not about luxury or exclusivity. They're for everyday use, designed to be worked in. "A serious pair of jeans," Eric called them. In his professional estimation, like wine, his jeans get better with age.

Working with Eric was exciting because we weren't making just any pair of jeans. We were making *my* pair. He sized me up instantaneously: 36 waist, straight leg, a boot cut with a slight flare. The answers sprang out of him automatically. My body and my personality became a specific pair of jeans in his mind. (On *A Craftsman's Legacy*, I worked with Nate Funmaker, a fur and felt hatmaker, who said this was the fun part, figuring out what someone's hat was. Customers invariably say they don't know what hat is right for them. "I don't know either . . . " he says. "Let's find out.")

In a small workroom, Eric and I began by unraveling a long roll of dark blue denim onto a table. Next, we took a paper layout of my pants size to trace on the denim in fine white chalk. Then we grabbed a powered rotary cutter, which Eric called a "Chickadee," to cut the denim along the white lines. From there we joined up with Eric's business partner and co-owner, Brenna Lane, for the rest of the process.

When I sat down with her, I had that moment where it clicked for me how little I knew about what we were doing. When I don't know a single thing about something, I often think it's more basic than actually it is. But once I get a glimpse behind the curtain of how it all works, I truly understand how much I don't know.

As I sat down with Brenna in front of the *twenty-seven* different parts of a single pair of jeans, I got that glimpse. In a million years I wouldn't have guessed there were that many. (Even the fly is made up of three separate parts and comes together in what they call a "fly taco.") I wear jeans pretty much every day, but they might as well have grown out of the ground for all I knew about them.

Besides the twenty-seven parts, it also takes ten different machines to make one pair of jeans. Each pocket requires four steps, involving various types of stitching, steaming, ironing, and sewing. The whole process is very dynamic and requires a high level of concentration and hand-eye coordination. We were constantly adjusting our hands and the drag we applied to the material as the sewing machines blazed on. It was fascinating getting to do it (poorly) and watching Eric and Brenna, who were locked into the machines. But I really enjoyed working in there, with the high ceilings and large windows looking out onto the city, the smooth feel of the fabric, the steam from the irons, the rhythmic clatter and clacking of the metal machines. It was old-school in the best way possible.

ERIC'S STORY IS inspiring, and his desire to build something individual reminded me of my own path. What drove me to become a metal shaper was not only that I wanted to make motorcycles. It was that I wanted the freedom and control of starting from the bottom and building up. If I could dream it, I wanted to be able to make it. Otherwise, I wasn't going to feel like it was really mine. Using someone else's fuel tank meant that the rest of my design—and the build that resulted—was limited, in some ways, by their concept. No matter how skilled you are, you can't turn a hamburger patty into a T-bone.

A litmus test I still give myself is when someone familiar with my work sees a Voodoo motorcycle, will they recognize it as one of mine? My principles of design are consistent and carry through from bike to bike, like a signature. A furniture maker I met in season four, Mark Whitley, described his portfolio this way: "Every piece looks different, but you can tell the same guy built them all." That's the ideal.

In the bike making industry, there is a healthy dose of self-promotion—people showing off their bikes to crowds to win acclaim and trophies. I understand that some people have that impulse, but it was never my thing. Turning the work into a contest, giving a judge the power to say what was best, has always seemed beside the point to me. It's also a double-edged sword, because having people see your work is wonderful, but with every compliment comes a critique. For me, a negative response will always massively outweigh a positive one. So I avoid those shows altogether.

I want a motorcycle to open up my understanding of what a bike can do, how the pieces fit together, what is possible with the machine. What is gained by taking things away? What is lost by adding? It's an internal process, a personal one. I want to be able to see something different about a bike every time I look at it. I might put a detail in it that only one out of a hundred people would notice—but *I* would notice. That's what matters to me.

When beginning work on a custom bike, I first figure out what style the customer wants, which drives the whole build. At Voodoo Choppers, what we usually make breaks down into three types: choppers, which have a long front end and skinny wheel; bobbers, which have a short rear fender and stubby front end; and diggers, which are long and low. Early on, I need to know how the customer likes to ride—aggressive, laid back, or two-up (with a passenger). Not everyone is concerned about passenger comfort, but if they are, that will change the design considerably. Then we talk about how they're going to use it. Is it for day trips with the spouse or for solo riding on quick trips nearby? Is this a garage queen or something they're going to put serious miles on?

Some customers get a bike because they want a reason to hit the open road next summer or they want to bring it to a rally like in Sturgis, South Dakota, the biggest bike event in America. Others are realistic and admit they're looking for a T-N-T bike—tavern to tavern. A T-N-T bike is for someone to take around to the local bars; they park out front and chat with their buddies, and then they roll down the street a couple of miles to another one and do it again. Not everyone can be a road king, grabbing miles and hitting the wind. Some riders' enjoyment of the bike is primarily the social aspect, the attention, and the community around it. I've always admired the community aspect of bikers. I've had many great times just sitting around and talking with guys about bikes, and I can do it for hours, with nowhere to go and nothing else to do.

In making their bike, I also like to get to know the customers, to capture something intangible that will help them connect with it. Customers' desires are often intimately tied to who they are. I had one guy come in who was color-blind. His only request was that I build a bike that he could see the same way everyone else did, so I made it all in blacks, whites, and grays. The bikes I make are handcrafted specifically for someone, so they make sense only for that person, like the way Eric Yelsma designed my jeans. Of course, the final bike is not just their personality, but mine as well—it's a combination, or rather a conversation between the two of us.

In general, though, I usually let the client guide me. Beauty is in the eye of the beholder, so I give them options, offer them pros and cons, and help them make their own decisions. But some customers want to be surprised. They don't want to see pictures at all—they just want to show up when it's ready and drive it off.

Part of the thrill of my work is bringing to life something that has never existed. But once it's done, I have to give it away. It was never mine to begin with. That's another one of the contradictions of being a craftsman—putting my heart and soul into it, thinking about it in my sleep and spending my days with it, and then letting it go.

16: A SPECIAL KIND OF STUPID

In the summer of 1998, months of being trapped inside my house—and in my mind—forced me to take a step back. I kept thinking back to that talk with my psychiatrist, about what I would do if money or time or nothing else mattered. The answer was the same, shining as clearly and vibrantly as that stained glass hanging from my window. I wanted to learn to build motorcycles, those majestic machines that had fascinated me since childhood. And I wanted to be the driver of my own life.

Slowly, I started to take the idea of building bikes—as a career—more seriously. At the time it was hard for me to know how realistic it was. In the vulnerable state I was in, my psychiatrist could've told me I needed to be an astronaut and go to Mars and I would've seriously considered it. I was that lost and desperate.

But I also had a feeling, a sense that a life of building bikes would be enough to sustain me, to feed my soul. The more I thought about it, the more it seemed possible. It felt like stepping through the fog and finally seeing the texture and shape of what I wanted to be.

After a few months on disability I returned to Xerox, in a part-time capacity, but I was changed and everyone could tell. I had a lot more quirks than I'd had before. I stopped wearing ties because I felt like they were choking me, got rid of my watch because I felt I was too dependent on time, and was a more fragile person all around. I wouldn't fly anywhere for jobs, had trouble driving, was still heavily medicated, and struggled being around people. All the while I continued on with something like a plan forming in my head. It felt liberating to have one.

The world had been kicking me down, and the only choice I had was to strike out on my own. I just didn't know how. So, in an effort to do something bold, to create a shock to my system, I filed paperwork with the state of Michigan to license the name for my not-yet-existent business: Voodoo Choppers. It was a huge gesture, like betting a stack of chips on myself.

When I told friends and family my plans, they were dumbfounded. *Why would someone with anxiety problems start their own business? How is that a good idea?* At that time I could barely talk to people for any length of time. I couldn't go out to dinner and had trouble on simple errands to the store. *How in the world is this going to help you?*

No one took this position more firmly than my dad. He assured me that I would never make it, that I was going to be broke, that I was a fool for trying. As a father myself, I can now see he was hoping to protect me, concerned about me making a living with my issues. There is a tremendous amount of stress that comes with running your own business, which he was all too aware of.

The responses bothered me, but I also knew that building anything on your own takes a special kind of stupidity. That's the only way to get something off the ground when there's no evidence that it will work. You have to be a little bit stupid, or at least bullheaded. Anyone who has gone out independently has had to come up against that doubt—it's one of the reasons people are averse to doing it. But making Voodoo Choppers a reality wasn't about telling others off or even proving them wrong. It was about refusing to let anyone else hold my star.

I knew how to fix up bikes, but so did a lot of people. I wanted to be able to create something original, not be tied down by others' ideas or decisions. In order to get there, the first thing I needed to do was to learn how to shape metal.

But I had come up against a wall. I'd already bought and read every book I could find, scoured every magazine and picture and manual. In the days before YouTube, that was about as far as you could go on your own. I could read all I wanted about it, but until I got hands-on experience, throwing hammers and tracking on a wheel, all that reading was going to be two-dimensional and inert.

I needed someone to take me on.

One Saturday, at my cousin's house to help with some remodeling, I was flipping through a *Hot Rod* magazine. In the back pages was a tiny classified ad for a metal shaping workshop with a man named Ron Fournier. I didn't connect it at the time, but he was renowned in the trade, the author of a couple of popular metal shaping books, which were integral to bringing the craft to the masses. The address for the shop was in Troy, Michigan, not five minutes from my house. It felt like a sign—opportunities don't always present themselves so bright and glaring. Here was a legend, and he was in my neighborhood.

On Monday I swung by the Troy shop after work, looking to poke around. I was just getting back to being around people, still a little skittish. At the front desk a young woman introduced herself as Ron's daughter Nicole. Though the shop was busy, she was friendly and spoke with me for a while, telling me about the classes. I mentioned that I had seen the ad. I didn't say so, but classes were not what I was looking for. Something about taking classes felt too small, too slow.

"Actually, would it be okay if I just looked around?" I asked. "I promise not to touch anything."

"Sure thing," she said. "Just don't bother Ron."

So I wandered in—and it was like walking into a dream. I had never been in a metal fabrication shop before, and it was exhilarating, like all those pictures come to life: hot rods, rare cars, a motorcycle with handmade skirted fenders, machinery whirring, guys shaping and banging on panels, the zipping sound of pneumatic grinders spinning on metal, exhaust fans humming from the paint booth.

In the back was an older man, short and stout with forearms like Popeye's, laying out metal. I strategically made my way over to him. "Are you Ron?" I asked.

"I am," he said. I introduced myself and told him I was interested in learning how to shape metal. He was solemn and quiet but enormously kind, far kinder than he needed to be, considering I was just some guy off the street. We hit it off immediately, like old friends, chatting for a while about cars and motorcycles. Ron loved racing, and could talk excitedly and intelligently about anything with a motor. I wore my eagerness on my sleeve and let him know I wanted to learn how to shape metal—from him. "Well, maybe you should take some classes first," he said.

"Yeah," I said, trying to avoid the topic. "To be honest, I don't really have the money for that kind of thing. I was thinking maybe I could work for you?" I started listing all the things I could fix, what I knew about bikes, but he told me they weren't hiring at the moment.

"Oh sure, I get it," I said, not really fazed. Against my typical shyness—what had become my armor over that year—I pushed forward. I could sense this was going to be it. Ron was my way in.

"Do you mind if I come by again though?" I asked.

"Sure thing," he said. "No problem."

I stopped by Ron's shop a few days later, and then a couple of days after that. Pretty soon I was swinging by a few times a week, before and after work. I would just hover around and ask questions, offer to help, listen and watch him shape thin gauge sheets on the English wheel or throw hammers into shot bags.

Looking back I see that I was a pain in the ass, eating up a lot of time, and not buying anything—three strikes against me. But to Ron's credit, he never made me feel like I was a problem. It's a testament to the way Ron saw his craft. He had no issue sharing it, especially with someone who was obviously desperate to learn. I think he could tell I wasn't just a hobbyist, that I was someone looking for a life change.

After a few months, I was even coming by on my lunch break from Xerox, still offering to help out, just emphasizing that I wanted to learn. Somehow I knew this would be my salvation and at some point he'd give in. Which, eventually, he did.

Almost a year after I met Ron I stopped in the shop one afternoon and he said, "Just the man I wanted to see."

"Oh yeah?" I said.

"Yep. We've got a big job coming up and we're looking to bring on another apprentice." Then, with a little jest in his voice, "Do you know anyone who might be interested in that?" He flashed me a smile.

That night I typed up my resignation from Xerox. Two weeks later, I was in Ron's shop ready to get to work. Though I was excited, the change was enough to make my ears bleed. With nothing but a high school education, I had been making a good salary at Xerox, with benefits, stock options, and paid vacations. And I left it all to work for Ron for eight dollars an hour, a fine selection of floor brooms, and an opportunity to learn from the best.

Through the various projects he had in the shop, Ron taught me basic skills: how to lay out a design on metal, how to bend a piece of metal using a brake, how to use a lathe, how to weld and file, and how to use a pneumatic grinder, which files faster. Ron taught me that metal shaping comes down to controlling shrinking and stretching, which happen at the same time; it's an elemental way to look at the process. If I pull a rubber band tight, I'm making it longer and thinner—that same principle applies to metal.

Ron taught me how to approach, measure, and reproduce a piece of metal, how to track on an English wheel, controlling the metal as it moves forward and sideways between the wheels, which takes serious practice. When I made a mistake, I'd instinctively apologize, and he would tell me not to, that this was an essential part of learning the craft. "The only difference between you and me, Eric" he said, "is I've made more mistakes than you."

Ron was a master at visualizing, and he instinctively understood how to correct issues. I've since worked with metal guys who will explain what's happening to the metal from a molecular structure standpoint. It's fascinating but not always useful in the moment. Ron cut right to the quick. "This is what's going to happen," he'd say, and if you asked why, he'd say, "Because I've done this for twenty years and when I do that this is what happens." It's like how I know the sun comes up every day because of the Earth's rotation. But also, I'm forty-six years old, and every single day of my life, that's what has happened.

Once you finally discover what you want to do—and can feel it within your grasp—everything else falls by the wayside. I offered to work as much as Ron would let me. When he went home for the day I'd stay late and practice welding and using other machines on metal scraps lying around. It was all about getting those hours under my belt as soon as I could. In my mind, I had already wasted enough time; I had to start making a living.

Getting thrown into the deep end is one way you learn to swim. That's why failure is so important. You only know how to fix things from messing them up in the first place. If you're afraid to fail, then you'll never get anywhere. I know a basketball coach who talks about dribbling drills and says that if you don't lose the ball at some point, then you haven't learned anything. Losing, breaking, falling, and failing are how we shape ourselves.

A FEW MONTHS into my apprenticeship, Nicole came over to me one day in the shop. "Listen, Eric," she said. I could tell by her tone that it was going to be bad news. "That big job we were supposed to get fell through."

"Oh," I said. "That's too bad."

"Yeah, it is. Look," she said, hesitating for a beat, "I'm sorry, but we can't pay you any longer." I'm sure she felt bad for me, and though I understood—business was business—the news was still a shock. I'd already thrown away my career and its security to do this, and now it was being snatched away.

It was a crossroads moment. I could've gotten my job back at Xerox, and I actually had a few other tech job offers. But having come that far, retreating wasn't an option for me. I told Ron I didn't care about the money. "I just want to continue learning," I said. "How do I do that?"

"I'll tell you what," he said, "if you can find work on your own you can use the shop for anything you need. And if you can help me out with my jobs I can keep teaching you. When you sell something, I'll help you make it." He gave me his blessing, a key to the shop, and access to all his equipment. It was the ultimate act of generosity.

Now I just needed to find some work.

I started to solicit business for myself, literally door to door. I would travel to mechanic shops, dealerships, and motorcycle businesses in the area and sell my services. I'd find out what parts they needed and offer to make them. By that point I had made a few things on my own, a couple of gas tanks and a fender, which I'd take around like copies of my résumé.

"Hi, my name's Eric," I'd say. "I started a business and I'm hand making parts. Do you have a need for anything like that?" I also carried around pictures of my own bike, an FXR that I was working on. During that period, I hustled like mad, hitting every shop and dealership in the greater Detroit area, hearing a ton of *no*s and *not right now*s. But I also met a lot of people in the trade, learned what people needed, and got my name out there in that time-honored way.

The arrangement with Ron was a scrappy and nontraditional one, which seemed like an extension of our friendship. I was using Ron's shop and my own garage, where I had accumulated a few pieces of equipment, and started to advertise Voodoo Choppers in local free circulars and through word of mouth at swap meets. It was a complete trial by fire, taking on projects that were *way* over my head and far past my skill set, pulling time estimates out of thin air, overselling my abilities, and undercharging for the jobs. Not really knowing what to quote, I didn't want to be turned away, and I had to answer on the spot. After I took on a job, Ron would help me through it. The entire normal progression was folded back on itself. I was learning and selling my work at the same time.

Eventually, Ron and Nicole, who had become like family, had to shut down their shop right around the time I had outgrown my garage. With no savings and a bank loan, I opened up a commercial space for Voodoo Choppers and bought some machines from Ron. Our relationship shifted and he would now come over to my space and help out. Soon Ron got a big job and needed a space to work in; I was happy to give back, while also continuing to learn. He and I were living that grand cycle, feeding back into each other.

Working with my hands, setting my own schedule, and having control over my environment did wonders for my anxiety. In hindsight, the solution I came up with was simple. I expanded my garage safe zone into my job, and then it filled up my life.

Ron eventually moved out and Voodoo Choppers took off. I added equipment and brought on part-time help, which became full-time, and it grew from there. It wouldn't have happened without Ron and Nicole's kindness and openness. And it wouldn't have happened if I had listened to pretty much anyone else. I ignored the people who said it couldn't be done, and just plowed through, certain of where I was headed. It was an attitude that emerged after a long time of being trapped—in my home and in my mind. I finally decided I wanted control over my future, and to get to that point, I tapped into something essential: that special kind of stupid.

17: CONNECTION

Having human hands and human discernment creating the products in an expert way—that's why we view chocolate as a craft. —JAEL RATTIGAN, *chocolatier*

In downtown Asheville, North Carolina, a homey place of brick-lined streets and sidewalk musicians, sits French Broad Chocolate Lounge. Its exterior is a bright blue that makes it pop out from the rest of the building. The place is owned and run by Dan and Jael Rattigan, a married couple whose remarkable journey to this spot is unlike anything I've ever heard. It can only be described as a craftsman's fairy tale, as romantic a story as I've come across in all my interviews, travels, and searches. Not in terms of the romance between two people—though that's there too—but between people and a dream. And it was all triggered by a fleeting moment that easily could have slipped by.

About ten years ago in Minneapolis, Jael was in business school with eyes on becoming an event planner, pretty certain which way her life was headed. On a date with Dan, who was feeling his way through law school, the couple found themselves in Jael's kitchen rolling chocolate truffles and caramels, confections Jael regularly made for friends and family.

Up to her arms in melted chocolate, lost in the rhythmic and meditative movement, Jael felt a tingling sensation in her hands. It was strange and inexplicable, and had never happened before. She held her hands out in front of her and stared at them, as though in a trance. What came out her mouth were the words that would change her life. "This is it," she said. "Chocolate will make me happy."

In that instant, she knew what she should be doing. "I was searching for fulfillment," she told me about that day, "and that gave me a glimpse of what it could be made of."

She and Dan had only been dating for a few months, but the experience fused them together, solidifying a bond that was new but already intense. Dan is an incredibly focused guy and took her seriously, not laughing her off or offering reasons not to pursue her dream. So Jael's moment became *their* moment; he stepped into her dream with her. And they decided to follow where it led. Jael's revelation released an energy into the air, and she gave it language, but it needed to be nurtured and supported to be kept alive. It had to be given oxygen.

For Dan and Jael, the only way to follow this passion was all the way. They dropped out of their respective graduate schools, got married, and sold everything they owned. The goal was to move down to Costa Rica, the headwaters of the chocolate world, where they purchased an abandoned cacao farm. To get there, they bought a school bus, converted it into an RV that could run on vegetable oil, and drove 3,500 miles south—drastically removed in so many ways from their graduate school lives in Minneapolis. They completely shut down their old life, took each other's hands, and rebooted it together.

Costa Rica is where their fairy tale would become a reality. Their plan was to park the bus on their new land and make it their home. But life intervened. A few days before they left Minnesota, they found out Jael was pregnant. Practicality prevailed and they redirected, opting to move instead to a beach town on Costa Rica's Caribbean coast. They pulled their bus in front of an outdoor restaurant space and eventually opened a café called Bread and Chocolate.

The Rattigans spent two years there, blessed with the rare opportunity to learn about the culture and history of the place and the product, to visit the cacao-rich jungles, and to learn from the people who lived and worked there. They built a life on a ground made from chocolate, giving their dream the room to breathe and spread out and bloom. In a short period of time they had transformed the tingling in Jael's hands into a purpose and a way of life.

I can't imagine anything more romantic.

THE *Theobroma cacao* plant was first popularized by the Mayans of southern Mexico and present-day

Guatemala and Belize. (Recent archeological evidence has shown that the Olmec civilization of southern Mexico actually discovered it as early as 1500 B.C.) *Theobroma* literally translates as "food of the gods." The Mayans ground the beans into a paste, flavored the paste with ingredients like chili peppers, and made a hot, foamy drink. It was a delicacy reserved for those of high status, a much more bitter version of the treat we know and love today. It was so valued that people traded the cacao beans as currency, drew and painted versions of them on artifacts, and used the drink for social and religious rituals.

Later, the Aztecs were also taken by the drink, which they enjoyed cold. They called it *xocolatl* (which translates as "bitter water" and which became the English word "chocolate.") After discovering it couldn't grow too far north into Mexico* they traveled the one thousand miles south to bring the beans back home.

In the sixteenth century, when explorers brought cacao back to Spain and the rest of Europe, sugar was added to the drink and the chocolate taste we'd recognize was born. With the industrialization of the mid-eighteenth century, machines and factories were able to make mass-produced chocolate. The first chocolate bars were made in England by Joseph Fry in 1847, followed by John Cadbury's version two years later. Soon after, milk and other ingredients were added to the recipe, and the industry as we now know it flourished.

---

* It grows in tropical climates, where there's humidity, rainfall, and light; the strip that runs within 20 latitude degrees from the equator is now called the "Chocolate Belt."

AFTER TWO YEARS in Costa Rica, with a child and the accompanying desire to put down roots, the Rattigans sold their café and moved to Asheville to start their own chocolate business. (They kept the farm, which has recently begun producing beans.) Their business began as a farmer's market brand out of their kitchen but soon moved to a space where they could "create an entire experience" around chocolate, where people could sit, savor, and socialize—a community that went beyond the typical fleeting, commercial transaction. The place did well, but something was missing. In buying chocolate from producers with whom they felt no connection, there was a troubling gap. Their experience in Costa Rica lurked like a remnant in their minds. And they were looking to re-create it.

So they decided to go from "bean to bar"—making craft chocolate—a time-consuming and intensive process practiced by only about two hundred companies in the United States. It's chocolate's version of farm to table. Instead of buying premade chocolate, now they buy the beans and make their own. Cacao grows on the plant in football-shaped pods, and the bags of chocolate beans, also called seeds, arrive at the Rattigans' in giant sacks. Dan and Jael sort the seeds, winnow them down (separating nibs, which they want, from the husk, which they don't), mill them, mix them into a paste in a stone refiner, add sugar, mash it into a liquid, temper it (bringing it up and then down in temperature), then melt it again and mold it into bars.

Their goal was not just to make chocolate; they wanted to educate the public on the chocolate's origins, similar to the movement that has happened over the last decade or so with coffee. Dan and Jael wanted to highlight and embrace the relationships that helped bring the chocolate about—both as a business practice and as a matter of the soul. They believed that the energy that is put into the food "conveys into the food and people's experience of the food," as Dan explained. Once they switched to going from bean to bar, they were closer to the business they had envisioned.

"We fit into a bigger picture of farmers and makers who have the same mission to bring integrity and intention back into the food and beverage that we consume," Jael told me. The Rattigans recognize that they are one link in a long chain and that they can positively affect others along that chain—from the farmers in Central America who plant the seeds, to those who harvest them, to those who ferment and dry and export and import and store the product.

Though it brought this "gift from the gods" to the public, and often in environments that could never naturally grow it, corporate chocolate has separated the consumer from the source and has introduced conformity to it. It had been a treasure for centuries, but in a short time, we've turned it into just another widget. "We've removed the sacred," Jael told me.

There's also a natural taste difference in chocolate that Jael and Dan are interested in highlighting. Each batch of beans is altered by the location, weather, farmers, soil, and hundreds of other factors. "We celebrate the difference, rather than driving just for consistency's sake." A Hershey bar tastes the same wherever you buy it, and that's the point.

When I got home from Asheville and ate some of the Rattigans' confections (hazelnut, which is my kryptonite), it was so much more of a unique experience than I'd ever had with chocolate, or any food really. Because I understood how it was made and where it came from, I paid attention to what I was eating, savored all its flavors and complexity. And it tasted like you'd expect something handmade with love to taste. I realized that I was the last link in a long chain that had traveled thousands of miles and has lasted thousands of years.

18: PURPOSE

I want to live a peaceful life, and I want to add beauty to the world. Those are really my only two goals.
—MARK WHITLEY, *furniture maker*

For so many craftsmen, the work is never just work. It can't be. It's a livelihood, a perspective on the world, a strong belief system, and a life's purpose. When I met Mark Whitley I immediately thought of a line by famed author and woodworker James Krenov about how a true craftsman expresses "their philosophy of living" through their work. That's Mark.

Mark worked in a factory for a spell but then began building furniture in the tiny back room of his dad's hardware store. It clicked for him in a way that was almost biological. After years of wavering and uncertainty, he felt like he was finally standing still. He could feel it: Building things was in his blood.

Once Mark discovered studio furniture, a movement that first sprang up in the 1940s as a response to the mass-produced mainstream, he knew he'd found what he looking for: his purpose. The studio furniture movement favored small and intimate work that infused art into craftsmanship. It was a world where furniture makers spent a long time on a single chair or table and it was "okay to have a great reverence for the material," Mark explained to me. It was there that he laid down roots and made a home.

Mark is rail thin with long straight hair and a very cool Rasputin-like beard. He has expressive eyes and a deep, syrupy drawl, relaxed as though nothing could ever rattle him. He grew up on a Kentucky farm with a dad who was a woodworker himself. From a young age Mark would spend time in his dad's shop "hacking away," as he described it. After high school Mark headed to Southern California for college, with a backpack and a guitar. He came out four years later with a degree in peace studies, which is a political science major that explores cultures and religions. After graduation he moved to Montana, where he landed a job in the youth ministry, figuring he would head to the seminary. But he eventually sensed the church wasn't for him and returned to the small town of Smiths Grove, Kentucky.

Nowadays Mark lives and works only a few miles from where he grew up, and almost exclusively builds on his own. It's a time-consuming process, but Mark has found joy and peace there—and it suits him just fine. He told me he exists a good deal on the barter system, trading away unsold items for various things around his house and shop. It's an older and simpler way of living, more connected to the community.

There's a personal connection between people and their furniture, and Mark understands part of his purpose is getting to know who and what he's building for. "It's the responsibility of the maker to create something that's not all about me," he told me. "It's about making something that will last for generations, and it being *right*." Part of his process is going to the place or room where his furniture will live and taking it all in. Then he goes back to his shop and tries to "blend what they've got going on with what's in my brain, and the movements and the curves that I've worked on for years, and sort of melt all that together."

His house, which he built himself, is a pretty amazing A-frame inside of which everything is handmade, from the lights to the furniture. It's part rustic and part steam punk, and as you'd expect, it's an extension of Mark's personality. On the bottom floor is his studio, with all kinds of saws and files and a poster of young Burt Reynolds in a cowboy hat above his workbench.

When we went into the studio, Mark and I worked on the base of one his signature tables, called a twist table. The idea came about from a commission he got to make a table for an Emmy award, the statue handed out for television shows. The Emmy statue has a globe with a helical shape at the top and Mark wanted the table to interact with that form, to give the impression that the whole piece was rising out of the ground. The table's base has these beautiful upward swooping curves that loop around each other, connoting "grace and movement," in Mark's words.

Mark's furniture is wholly unique, with shapes and curves reminiscent of sculpture far more than furniture. His pieces are fluid, with minimal use of hard or straight lines; he likes to play around with twists and turns and organic shapes that you normally don't see in furniture. The effect is to keep your eyes moving over the piece, bringing it a sense of motion and flow. It comes alive.

Incredibly, Mark doesn't use any steam to bend his wood. When I first saw the curves in his pieces, I assumed he did. That's the only way I'd ever seen it done, but Mark's process was new to me. First, he sawed cherry wood planks into long thin strips. Then he glued seven of the strips together, creating what's called a lamination (the term for any layers or boards glued together), and while the glue was wet, he twisted the pliable pieces into a curve. Then he set it into place with a bunch of clamps, and eight hours later the glue , had dried and the unreal curves of wood stayed in place.

Mark was a fountain of knowledge. He understood so much about chemical properties and the reactions of various materials, oxidizers, woods, and glues. One of my favorite tricks he did to his wood was ebonizing, which is a century-old method of darkening wood. He puts steel wool into a jar with vinegar and tanic acid, and after three days he has this tea-looking solution. When he rubbed the wood of the table base with this mixture, it started to change color before our eyes, like a Polaroid coming to life. By the time it was done, it looked like black iron.

Impressively enough, Mark's finished pieces don't contain a single nail, screw, or metal fastener of any kind. He used dowels (wooden pegs) to fit on a tabletop of ambrosia maple. The wood came from a nearby tree that blew down in a storm—two years ago. It was a such a long process because he had to air-dry the wood, and that takes a year per each inch of thickness. Though Mark's work has an almost modernist slant, it still has a rustic, back-to-nature ethos. He loves getting in touch with the wood's natural state in that way and once made a conference table from a giant tree stump, which took him a full year to complete.

The church didn't end up becoming his future, as he had thought it would, but it did end up returning to him, in yet another example of a craftsman's full circle. Mark's handmade Communion tables became popular and have ended up in churches across America—from Kentucky to Kansas to California. Mark has the kind of intelligence that spreads from the technical to the spiritual; he has a firm grasp of his purpose, which goes beyond his material. Wood is simply the medium with which he serves the world.

Mark and I got to talking about purpose and how to know if you've reached yours in life. "I'm doing what I'm supposed to be doing," he said. "Because if this isn't what I'm supposed to be doing, society is going to tell me that. And then I'll do something else." Mark touched on something that I had thought about but never was able to so succinctly explain: The universe will let you know one way or another if you are where you should be. It's up to you whether or not you listen, whether or not you want to keep going further down that road. Ultimately, I believe we end up where we are meant to be.

I think of Wilson Capron, who ran into engraved spurs while on his way to pay for his dream of being a rodeo cowboy. Or Eric Yelsma, who lost his job and couldn't get his tailor to make him a new pair of jeans. At eighteen, Mark left his Kentucky home, traveled out West, learned about the world, saw some of it, and then returned—less than five miles away from where his grandfather started, doing the thing his father did, his history curling back in on itself.

When you find your purpose, you still shoulder worries like anyone, but at least the grand question *What am I doing here?* feels answered. Or addressed for now. That path felt so right for Mark that he told me, "Everything about my career, it's almost as if I never had any choice."

> **Clay and fire are my partners. We collaborate.**
> **I am the producer ... each clay comes out completely**
> **different because each one has its own personality.**
> —AKIRA SATAKE, *potter*

ONE AFTERNOON I found myself sitting across a small glass table from Akira Satake, cups of tea in front of each of us, watching him play banjo. His eyes were closed as he plucked a lilting and mesmerizing melody. The banjo, which I'd always associated with a certain kind of playful country sound, was soulful, almost melancholy, in Akira's hands. It was some of the most beautiful music I've ever heard. Lost in the moment, I'd almost forgotten that I wasn't there to listen to Akira play banjo.

Akira Satake was born in Osaka, Japan, and made his way to Tokyo, then San Francisco, and finally to New York City as a young man with dreams of becoming a photographer.

He'd been playing the banjo on the side, an instrument he'd always loved. (The banjo was so foreign in Japan that Akira and his brother had to re-create one from a photograph.) Eventually, in the way that Mark Whitely described, the universe directed him what to do. With no photography jobs in the offing, Akira would wander to Washington Square Park to play his banjo. There he met a group of musicians with whom he started playing—live and in studio sessions. Years of this led to a job running a recording studio in Midtown Manhattan and then owning a record company. He was a success—in the place where it's hardest to become one—but there was a problem. He wasn't at peace.

At age forty-two, finding himself buckling under all the stress and unable to sleep, he searched for a way to relieve the tension and landed on a pottery class. In his first class, he said to himself, "I think I'm going to do this for the rest of my life." He smuggled out a half bag of clay to work on at home, often during those late hours when he couldn't sleep.

As he learned and refined this new craft, Akira realized producing other people's music had been sucking him dry. "It was like giving my ideas to each recording, I felt empty," he told me. "I didn't have time to feel *me* before I got empty." Pottery rescued him and eventually became his life.

Fifteen years later, Akira lives in Asheville, North Carolina, and is still creating his beautiful and unusual pottery, for which he often makes his own clay by putting ingredients in a pug mill mixer: kaolin (a type of clay mineral), silica, silica sand, feldspar (a rock mineral), granite, and water. He uses a wheel from time to time, but mostly what he does is pinch pottery, which is exactly what it sounds like. Pinching the sides and ends to create shapes—teapots, cups, plates, and sometimes sculpture. It's a technique that is deceptively complex, and doing it physically puts you inside of civilizations past.

Akira's work has such an organic look; the textures are rich in expression and the coloring comes from ash that melts onto the clay inside the kiln. All the scores on the pieces give them an aged look, like the work is centuries old. They have a primitive nature with an Asian influence, especially in the balance and simplicity of the design. It's very inviting to touch and feel.

Akira has a boyish mop of gray hair and an infectious, bright smile. After we finished our tea he took me to his studio. His approach to pottery has a spiritual bent, and he spoke to me about understanding the personality of the clay—how it reacts to his fingers, to being cut, to being fired. There's a distinguishing quality for each batch, and he has learned how to understand and make use of it. Though he has great reverence for the tradition that he is building on, he is committed to experimentation, the desire to throw different clays together and to try something new. "Every firing I need to do some part of it that's completely new," Akira told me. "Otherwise I don't move on to the next step."

As a teacher, Akira is also unconventional—steering his students to think for themselves. He tells his students not to listen to him, because if they do they might just make a copy of what he does, which is the last thing he wants them to do. Even when their choices lead to errors or dead ends, he remains enthusiastic. "Any mistake is 'Yeah! I never thought I would do such a thing,'" he said. "All those kinds of mistakes coming from ignorance or carelessness, it's wonderful."

It struck me as the inverse of traditional schooling, with its rote memorization, standardized tests, and incessant copying. Akira is hoping to impart something beyond that. He wants his students to learn to expand their minds and craft in a manner that could *only come from them*. His goal is to send them home "energized and excited and looking at their work from a different place and working with what they have." It's pottery as a means of discovery and self-discovery, just as had happened—and continues to happen—to him.

For Akira, achieving his pieces' desired look, texture, and color can take up to fifty hours, partly because the clay has to dry so slowly. Controlling the temperature is critical, which means that a wood-fired kiln requires a sentry to feed it every fifteen minutes—he has an assistant to help so he can get some sleep. That kind of patience may seem abnormal to some, but I'm happy that there are still people out there who care enough to do what it takes to get things right.

When I was with Akira, I got to witness the moment of truth that he both relishes and dreads. It was the day he was opening another kind of kiln, this one powered by natural gas, to see how his recent pieces had come out. Because of the serendipity and experimentation in his work, the relinquishing of control, the reveal is always a surprise. It could be a disaster, but that's the price of taking the risk. That trade-off is representative of how he has lived his life—from photography to music to pottery to whatever the future will bring. Akira is constantly searching for his purpose—but it's not a stagnant thing. He's got his ears and eyes open to the world.

Wanting to see what's around the bend, its twists and turns, is the common denominator with all the craftsmen I meet. So many of them have come up against something that caused them to reevaluate what they've been doing and look in a different direction. It reminds me that everything we do—even when it feels like we're going in the wrong direction—is leading it to the next stage. Often we have to pass through pit stops to reach the place where we feel like we should be, our purpose. Those weren't pit stops at all—they were stepping stones to a new version of ourselves.

19: A CRAFTSMAN'S LEGACY

*The place to improve the world is first in one's
own heart and head and hands, and then
work outward from there.* —ROBERT M. PIRSIG,
Zen and the Art of Motorcycle Maintenance

I never set out to be on television. It didn't seem to have anything to do with what I thought of then as my purpose, or even what I was good at. But I did have something to say, and television is still a great way to share a message. *A Craftsman's Legacy* was born through the combination of two thoughts that had been bouncing around in my head for some time.

The first came from inside my world. When you make things with your hands, you become part of a community—those you work with, you meet, you hear about. There's a kinship and a set of shared values; no matter how different the work, we're all connected. I'd hear these extraordinary stories of how people got into their craft, and I'd also be astounded by the quality and originality of their work. I knew in my bones that others would want to learn about them.

The second thought came from the outside world. Voodoo Choppers had a decent following, and I appeared on a few building contest television shows that brought more publicity to my shop. So I would get contacted by young people, older guys, guys in jail, people from all walks of life who wanted to get into bike building. But when I responded to them I found that they weren't doing anything to help themselves. Almost universally they put up barriers—*I don't have access to the gear, knowledge, tools, equipment*. They couldn't get past that first step. What I kept hearing was some version of *I could never do that*.

It frustrated me because I knew it wasn't true. I wasn't doing anything—*nobody* was doing anything—that someone else could not do if they put in the hours. I mean that sincerely. There's nothing supernatural going on in these shops: It's just the steady application of practice, passion, and time.

Of course, some people are more natural with their hands, or have excellent hand-eye coordination and dexterity, but I think those talents are not all that important in the grand scheme of things. Plus, they can be taught. You still have to learn to work with the materials, internalize the steps, and care enough to take your time and get it right.

So I started seeing that ignorance as a knowledge gap, even an opportunity. I wanted to turn closing that space into a mission. If people could understand that it was just dedicated men and women, putting in the hours with focus and humility and patience, getting up every day with an awareness of what they did and where they fit, maybe it would inspire others to step forward. Maybe it would encourage more people to work with their hands—if only in their free time and for themselves.

So the show was based on these notions—spreading the word about those who did and motivating others who wanted to do.

Getting it off the ground was a whole other matter. It took about five years, with a series of stops and starts, various helpful and not-so-helpful meetings with producers who had their own ideas, including one in California who wanted to get rid of me as host and turn it into a game show. (I said thanks, but no thanks.) I'd make some headway, get people interested in coming aboard, and then things would die out and it would go on the back burner. Putting together a television show is one of the most involved enterprises out there. It requires the right mix of ideas, people, luck, timing, and circumstances—and so much of it is outside your control.

Along the way, I learned a lot—from everyone. Sometimes you meet people who seem, on the surface, to provide poor information, advice, or feedback. You discard it, but in the end, you've learned what you *don't* want, which helps you define your own goals and direction. It's just like in craftsmanship, unearthing the lessons from mistakes.

Over those years I also met people who truly believed in me and the concept of the show. When you are doing something new and foreign to you, it's easy to find people who will tell you it can't be done or that you'll fail. These people are everywhere, and they always seem to come out of the woodwork when we are most vulnerable, like they did when I first started Voodoo Choppers. You have to make a conscious choice to surround yourself with people who believe in you and want to help. They're the angels hovering right beside you. I call them "the cherished few," and with their help we were able to make a pilot episode and shop the show around.

Some networks were interested, but I had formed an impression that when a network pays for the show, they are fully in charge. They might call it a partnership, but they get to screen all the casting and locations, and whatever they're not happy with, they can cut. I didn't want to work with a network that might suck out the spirit of the show, and I refused to lose the authority to dictate the content. Also, the idea was to highlight craftsmen and craftsmanship, not deal with product placement and manufactured drama. That stubbornness was important to making the show what it is, but it made it that much harder to get it on the air.

A Craftsman's Legacy eventually landed with American Public Television, which airs shows on PBS. They license the season for distribution, but we are independent producers who develop and make all the episodes. And the integrity of public television clearly fit with the type of show I aspired to make.

Now, THERE'S A reason people with histories of anxiety issues don't often host television shows. The night before my first on-camera interview, I was a mess, freaking out, just

a ball of jitters. I convinced myself that everyone was waiting to see me screw up and that they were right to think I
would. Any confidence I had in my ability to host was slowly
draining away as the clock ticked. *What the hell was I thinking?* I thought. *I can't do this.* I downed a couple of whiskeys
to calm my nerves, eventually fell asleep, and woke up before
the sun the next morning. My goal was to get through the
day without getting too lost in my head or letting down all
these people who had gone to bat for me.

The first part of the interview, with a woodworker in his
home, went smoothly. The only feedback was that I should
smile more, that I was appearing too serious. We broke for
lunch and then regathered in his shop to shoot the rest of
the sequence. But when I got back out in front of the cameras, microphones, and lights, something was off. I came out
like a bull in a china shop. Something about the setup gave
birth to this loud and boisterous version of myself, someone
who certainly didn't belong on the show. I could sense that
I was acting strangely, and the director immediately called,
"Cut." We tried it again, and that's when things got worse.

First, I made the mistake of looking at the crew looking
at me, instead of looking at the craftsman and interacting
directly with him. Then my mind started racing, and before
I knew it I was worrying about my appearance, whether
viewers would like me, and dozens of other concerns, which
set off a flash of panic: *Why am I doing this? I don't belong
here. I'm not a TV person.* Take after take, I just kept fumbling. It was a feedback loop, because each take I felt like
I was screwing up and people were watching me, and that

self-doubt got stuck in my head so it became impossible for me to get back on track.

I asked the director if we could take a break and talk outside for a moment. I needed to get fresh air, dig around for my confidence. It was an early December shoot in Michigan, so it was brisk and already dark in the late afternoon. My mood was bleak and I looked at the director for any reassurance. "Just be yourself," he said, over and over. It was the best advice I could've received.

We went back in and I made it through the rest of the shoot without much incident. If you watch that first episode, you can likely tell that I'm not totally comfortable. But it was my first time, and now I take it in stride. As I tell my daughter, no one is good at something when they first start out. I can't preach that all the time and be surprised that my first time doing something complicated—requiring me to juggle a bunch of conscious and unconscious things simultaneously and *look natural* while I do them—didn't go so smoothly. Hosting is a learned skill like anything else.

Since then, any success the show has had is a testament to the team that puts it together and the quality of craftsmen we've featured. Over the years the method of who we select to appear on the show and how we select them has become much more refined and thorough. It began off the cuff and casual—you could even say disorganized. Now there are preinterviews and meetings and plenty of preparation.

What our team is looking for in the craftsmen is a combination of things: their story, their work, their personality, and most importantly, their willingness and ability to share.

During our preinterviews, if craftsmen are too protective of their process, then we don't select them for the show. That's a strict rule that I feel strongly about. We've turned down some astoundingly talented people who didn't subscribe to a philosophy of openness about their work.

Another thing that makes it tricky is we're looking for authenticity, which doesn't always translate into someone who is comfortable on television. You could even argue those two qualities are at odds with each other. Most people are not natural on screen, because it is an inherently unnatural situation. Plus, we're sometimes featuring introverted men and women who spend a good deal of time on their own with their work. And we're asking them to be part of an illusion. For the viewer at home, it's designed to feel like a casual talk, but it's actually the opposite: cameras and lights packed in a small room; boom microphones dangling over our heads; crew members with walkie-talkies chatting about setups, light, and lenses. At the center of it all is a craftsman who is not used to being onstage.

We also tend to avoid self-promotional types, because they clash with the show's style and purpose. So we have to deal with that contradiction, the fact that we're running a TV show but we're not looking for people angling to be on TV. Sometimes we have to take into account how someone comes across or sounds, but I don't get too concerned with the details. I'm not perfect myself, we're not producing a reality show, and I like people who feel authentic, strong accents and all. I just want their intentions to be true. As much as it can be said of a television show, what you see is what you get.

A Craftsman's Legacy is a celebration, but it's also a demonstration, a lesson. If we simply showed the expert at work, then there'd be no connection there for the viewer. It'd be a passive experience. The fact that I'm trying to make an object, usually as a complete novice, gives the audience a way of see themselves trying it too. I'm a host in a literal sense; the viewer is vicariously experiencing it all through me. I'm not afraid to make an ass out of myself, ask a dumb question, admit I'm totally lost, or break something. That's by design.

In the shop, when the camera turns to film the craft portion, that's the first time I'm doing it. There's no practicing or trial work or fakery—it's as real as we can make it. Any cheating would undo the whole point of the show. The idea is to bring in the viewers at home, making them feel like they wandered in to this workshop and are getting an intimate and personal lesson.

For the craftsman, of course, I'm sure our crew feels a little intrusive. Nine of us show up—producers and directors, camera people, grips, sound guys—trampling through their house with our work boots, dragging through wires, using the restroom, taking over their space, scaring their pets. We cause a bit of a scene in some of these homes, which I can tell are relatively peaceful places before we barrel through the door. But I believe they know it's worth it. Most craftsmen are passionate about what they do and, like me, feel a responsibility to ensure their craft's future. The show has a purpose, and for me, it is a living entity. It has a spirit.

One of the great joys of making the show is watching the way people come to life when talking about their craft. It's like a certain question will turn a key that opens up their true selves. Other times they don't reveal as much during our on-camera interview, but once they get working, they come through in full stereo sound. That's how they communicate best. Not in direct conversation; they'd rather their hands do the talking.

These men and women are a part of America, integral to its creation and sustenance, and I can feel that history when I work alongside them. And I come out the other end with something. And maybe, if all goes well, the viewer does too. That's all I can hope for.

CONCLUSION: DAY ONE

I am an axe
And my son a handle, soon
To be shaping again, model
And tool, craft of culture,
How we go on.
—GARY SNYDER

Sometimes I need a break from the shop and the bikes and the machines and the noise but I still want to explore that creative urge. As a Catholic who loves wood and beautiful design, I've taken lately to carving crosses. They have long held a fascination for me: the physical design, the simplicity and elegance, the history and symbolic power.

In my travels around the country I'm always popping into antique stores to search for crosses, which I hang on two walls in my house. They're all different sizes, materials, and designs, and that's something I like about crosses: There's a wide variety, but they all maintain certain consistent principles. I have the metal and wood crucifix that was in my childhood bedroom, a tiny cross from Jerusalem carved out of olive wood, a Celtic-influenced oak one that I made with my granddad for my communion when I was eight. The foot that once stood it up is long gone, and the wood has warped, giving it a distinct curve. And I have a cross tattoo on my hand that will go with me to the grave.

The cross possesses an aesthetic grace that I respond to. One of my favorites is a simple wooden one with some light detail and a group of silk flowers in the center. My father gave it to my mom as a gift; when she passed away, it made its way down to me, and someday I'll give it to my daughter.

It was only recently that I actually started to making crosses, though I had thought about it for some time. About ten years ago I casually mentioned to a friend that I might like to carve and sell crosses in my free time. "No one's going to pay that much for a cross, Eric," she told me. "And you don't have time as it is, and you're going to put in all this time and not make money out of it." So that was that. I didn't really care about the money, but I figured she was right. I'd put the idea out there and it didn't get any traction. In hindsight, I should've followed my passion—just like with Voodoo and the TV show—but for whatever reason I was vulnerable and defenseless to that kind of negativity. So I let it die.

Over Christmas last year I had some pinewood left over from a picture frame I had made as a gift, and my mind flashed back to the cross. I cut some of the wood and carved one with a design that was suggestive of the body of Jesus. It wasn't overt, and I left it up to the eye of the observer: Some people see it as a body, and some don't.

I posted a photo of it on social media, and surprisingly, people asked if it was for sale. It wasn't the reason I put it up at all, but I figured, why not? Before I knew it I had twenty people on a waiting list. It had accidentally snowballed. Sometimes the world will surprise you like that.

So now I work on them in my free time, usually at night. I get lost in the process, learning by screwing up and steering myself back on track. That's part of the enjoyment: I don't really know what I'm doing. I don't consider myself an artist or a wood-carver, I have no experience in painting, and I can't draw well. But none of those seemed like a good enough reason not to do it. And once I actually began making the crosses, it became an affirming thing.

I made a few crosses with a burned finish, taking a torch to the wood and then rubbing it with steel wool to give it that distinctive look and color. Then I started experimenting with stains and gold and black spray paints. Those painted crosses, when they're done, look like they're made from iron or gold. I've taken only one special request, from a woman whose niece had passed away: one with an angelic figure in it, in her memory.

Within the basic shape of the cross there's a lot of room for improvisation and creativity. It's like recapturing that child-like desire to create. It also lays down more bricks on this ongoing path I've been on my whole life: *What can I make? What's next?* It doesn't end. Working with some of the most accomplished craftsmen in their fields and hearing their stories always drives this home to me: Everyone has a day one.

Just about every time we hear about an artist, actor, or athlete, we're learning about them at the pinnacle of their careers. The very fact that we're hearing about them means they've "made it." But we rarely account for the backstory. Someone blows up, and it seems like it's overnight, but if we were to go back and see them building toward that moment, we'd understand how incremental their development was. Does that mean that their work was terrible the week or day before they broke through? Of course not.

Craftsmen are no different. We know about them when their work becomes renowned. But we didn't hear about them years earlier when they were bartering their stuff, giving it away to relatives, or selling it on the sidewalk. By the time we find out about them they have put in so much work. All that work is the *reason* we're finding out about them.

It also doesn't mean that their work isn't worth buying before they reach that point. I try to persuade people to buy handmade, and they'll often say something like, *I'd love to but I really can't afford it. It's too expensive.* This is a common but entirely incorrect assumption. You might not be able to afford the best of the best, but there's a wide range of handmade. It's like saying because you can't afford a Bugatti you might as well walk everywhere, that you can't afford a filet mignon so you have to starve.

I try to keep in mind what Walter Arnold told me to do: *Look up.* Hiding in plain sight are all these beautiful and impressive examples of craftsmanship that we don't even notice. There are talented people everywhere. When I was in San Francisco for a PBS conference, I found a guy on the sidewalk selling beautiful hand-braided leather bracelets dyed in coffee. At a store they'd cost hundreds of dollars—I bought one for about thirty bucks, and now I wear it all the time. That cross from Jerusalem on my wall comes from a woman who was selling her goods on the street after church one day. If you know to look for it, you'll be amazed what you can find.

Even if we don't live in a place where artists are lined up selling their work, we all can get online. The Internet, though it has drawbacks, has helped individual craftsmen get their work noticed by anyone, anywhere. Or you can go to your local craft show or farmers' market. You can support these people, this world, and this way of life. Turn your appreciation into something concrete.

WE'RE LIVING IN an astounding time that historians will look back on with awe. Improvements in matters of convenience, speed, and entertainment have occurred at a remarkable rate. I recently read that when toddlers pick up magazines they use their fingers to try to enlarge the picture. That's the reality they know.

Technology has grown into an ever-present and all-powerful aspect of our lives, but when you become a slave to it, your balance is thrown off. Technology's great selling point, going back to the Industrial Revolution, was that humans would be freed up to do other things. Of course, that hasn't happened at all. It's the garage principle—no matter the size of your garage, you will always overfill it. I doubt that there's anyone in America who has an empty garage, room, closet, or drawer in their house. So despite our technological advances, we're busier than ever, our lives more frazzled. We're moving faster than we ever have. And we're also disregarding things as quickly as ever.

That's why the handmade object, created with care and detail, embodying a history and a tradition, is enormously powerful. It can cut through so much and speak in ways that we don't often hear, or that we've forgotten. Crafts and craftsmanship can move us, help us feel alive, and restore our sense of our humanity.

Shawn Messenger, the glassblower from Ohio, who we featured on an episode of *A Craftsman's Legacy*, told me she received an email from a customer of hers out of the blue late one night. He was a CPA and it was right around tax time. "I just want you to know that I'm sitting here trying to do everybody's taxes, and it's right at the end when everybody is driving me crazy, and I have your vase sitting on my desk. I'm trying to get all this done, and your vase actually . . . I look at it, and it takes me away for a minute, and then I can come back and continue on."

Shawn told me that story in passing and I often go back to it in my mind. It captures that deep connection a person can have with a piece of craftsmanship, an object that has been made with care and love, that was built through wisdom and experience, that can travel and touch whomever it comes in contact with. I feel like that's what I—and maybe all craftsmen—are motivated by. The idea of creating something that speaks.

APPENDIX

Featured Craftsmen

Jake Weidmann, Artist and Penman
https://www.jakeweidmann.com/

David MacDonald, Potter
http://davidmacdonaldpottery.com/

Alan Kaniarz, Woodworker
http://www.akservicesinc.com/

Alan Hollar, Wood Turner
http://piedmontcraftsmen.org/artist/alan-hollar/

Jim Gaster, Cooper
http://www.beaverbuckets.com/

David Riccardo, Metal Engraver
http://www.riccardoengraving.com/

April Wagner, Glassblower
https://www.epiphanyglass.com/

Seth Gould, Blacksmith
http://www.sethgould.com/

Walter S. Arnold, Stone Carver and Sculptor
http://www.stonecarver.com/

Wilson Capron, Bit and Spur Maker
http://wilsoncapron.com/

Maple Smith, Yarn Spinner
https://www.etsy.com/shop/NorthStarAlpacas#

Shawn Messenger, Glass Artist
https://www.artfulhome.com/artist/
Shawn-E-Messenger/7944

Nathan Bower, Clockmaker
http://www.bowerclocks.com/

Kevin Cashen, Swordsmith and Bladesmith
http://www.cashenblades.com/

Geri Littlejohn, Flutemaker
http://www.wicozaniflutes.com/

Bryan Galloup, Guitar Maker
http://www.galloupguitars.com/

Curtis Buchanan, Windsor Chair Maker
https://www.curtisbuchananchairmaker.com/

Noel T. Grayson, Arrow Maker
http://www.cherokeeheritage.org/

Eric Yelsma and Brenna Lane, Jeans Makers
https://detroitdenim.com/

Nate Funmaker, Hatter
http://www.nathanielsofcolorado.com

Dan and Jael Rattigan, Chocolatiers
https://www.frenchbroadchocolates.com/

Mark Whitley, Furniture Maker
http://mwhitley.com/

Akira Satake, Ceramist
https://akirasatake.com/

Jackie Wilson, Rocking Horse Maker
http://wilsonrockinghorses.com/
hand_made_rocking_horses/

Casmira Orlowski and Jeff Wagner, Fly Rod Makers
http://wagnerrods.com/

ACKNOWLEDGMENTS

PEOPLE ENTER YOUR life for many reasons. The people in this group are the ones who have picked me up when I've fallen, cheered for me in success, and continue to teach me to be a better man. I struggle to express in words the love and gratitude I have for all of these people in my life.

Mom: You taught me to love and respect people and always be there for them. Rest in peace, Mom.

Dad: I've never met anyone as tenacious and hardworking. You taught me to never give up and never be afraid to try something new. Love you, Dad.

Grandpa: I learned a lot about life and woodworking from you, especially patience. I miss spending time in your workshop, but the smell of sawdust brings me right back. Rest in peace, Gramps.

Chase: You are such a beautiful and full-hearted young lady. Follow your dreams and never give in. You give me strength and hope for tomorrow. I love you.

Scott: You've always been there for me. I miss those early days with Voodoo Choppers, doing shows and working all night.

Mark: Good times and bad times, you have helped me more than I can remember.

Thayer: You cared for me when I was sick and always supported me on my adventures. Thank you for being in my life. XO, E

Traci: Thank you for all the long conversations, love, and support. It would not have been the same without your love and never-ending support.

Rick Wade: Thank you for all the advice, guidance, and faith in me. It impacted my life more than you realize.

Jim Harper: I don't know how this would have happened without you. I've learned so much from you and can't thank you enough.

Jim Edelman: Thank you for the years of support. We have some great memories on the road filming.

Susan Venen-Bock: Thank you for believing in our show.

Selena Lauterer: You taught me a lot about public television and have always been a sounding board for my crazy ideas. Thank you.

Alison Fargis: Thank you for guiding me through this literary maze.

Jon Sternfeld: You are an amazing craftsman of words, my friend. Thank you for all the hard work.

Amy Gash: Thank you for taking good care of me and our book.

Algonquin: Thank you to the entire team at Algonquin for giving me an opportunity to share these stories.

NOTES

CHAPTER ONE

5   *A Japanese aesthetic called* wabi-sabi   http://www.wholeliving.com
/133628/wabi-sabi-your-life-6-strategies-embracing-imperfection

6   *The Navajo traditionally*   http://findingyoursoul.com/2012/06
/deliberate-mistakes/

12   *It remained the most popular*   http://sites.dartmouth.edu
/ancientbooks/2016/05/23/the-writing-instrument-the-reed-
and-quill-and-ink/

12   *With the increasing mechanization of*   https://www.britannica.com
/art/calligraphy

12   *Morris obsessively studied*   https://www.lib.umd.edu/williammorris
/morris-as-calligrapher

12   *it was a calligraphy class*   Steve Jobs's 2005 Stanford
Commencement Address, Princeton University

CHAPTER THREE

25   *Pitchers for carrying food*   http://ceramics.org/learn-about-ceramics
/history-of-ceramics

25   *The potter's wheel, which originally*   Samuel Noah Kramer,
The Sumerians: Their History, Culture, and Character (Illinois:
University of Chicago Press, 1963)

26   *Over time the pottery becomes*   http://ceramics.org
/learn-about-ceramics/history-of-ceramics

32   *The leftover attention from*   "Attention Residue" is discussed in
     detail in Cal Newport's *Deep Work: Rules for Focused Success in
     a Distracted World* (New York: Grand Central, 2016). It was first
     introduced as an idea by business professor Sophie Leroy in a
     2009 paper called "Why Is It So Hard For Me To Do My Work?"

CHAPTER FOUR

36   *Wood has been used to build structures*   https://www.bdcnetwork
     .com/history-building-wood-infographic

36   *back to when the first wood buildings*   https://www.logcabinhub
     .com/living-with-wood-from-the-beginning-of-time/

36   *From ancient Rome to Africa*   https://www.wagnermeters.com
     /woodworking-history/

38   *The movement is more natural*   https://www.popularwoodworking
     .com/american-woodworker-blog/japanese-dozuki-saws

41   *Known as the "mother of machine tools"*   https://www.jfberns.com
     /post/the-mother-of-machine-tools-part-one

41   *It was not until the Middle*   https://www.chestermachinetools.com
     /blogs/news/the-mother-of-machine-tools

CHAPTER FIVE

53   *two different languages*   I read something similar to this in Matthew
     Crawford's *Shop Class as Soulcraft* (Penguin Press, 2009)

54   *Historian Ian Mortimer*   https://www.fastcompany.com/3065643
     /how-the-invention-of-the-mirror-changed-everything

54   *Obsidian, a natural volcanic glass*   https://www.britglass.org.uk
     /history-of-glass

54   *The earliest version of man-made glass*   Ibid.

54   *The art of glassblowing was invented*   https://memoryglass.com
     /blog/index.php/history-of-glass-blowing/

54   *In fact, it was so highly secretive*   Ibid.

56   *Only about 10 percent of*   https://www.theatlantic.com/education
     /archive/2014/11/what-can-you-really-do-with-a-degree-in-the-arts
     /382300/

CHAPTER SIX

66 *"on a cycle you're in the scene"* Robert M. Pirsig, *Zen and the Art of Motorcycle Maintenance: An Inquiry into Values*, Mass Market Paperback (New York: Harper Torch, 2006), 4

CHAPTER SEVEN

77 *In fact, stone carvings are considered* https://stonecarversguild.org/

77 *To this day it remains one of the great* http://www.aeraweb.org/sphinx-project/geology-of-the-sphinx/

78 *They agreed on formal training* https://www.britannica.com/topic/guild-trade-association

79 *though air-driven chisels* https://sites.duke.edu/nashervirtue/stone-carving-history/

81 *Marble has been "the lifeblood"* *The Rough Guide to Tuscany and Umbria*, 10th edition, (Rough Guides, 2018)

82 *which the Renaissance master described as* https://www.reuters.com/article/us-italy-marble/michelangelos-unrealized-marble-dream-comes-true-in-italian-quarry-idUSKBN1AI1C1

83 *The functional aspect was to direct water* http://mentalfloss.com/article/88019/10-fearsome-facts-about-gargoyles

CHAPTER EIGHT

86 *To see anything in relation* Edith Hamilton, *The Greek Way* (Norton, 1964)

86 *Frank Shamrock, a mixed martial arts* Ryan Holiday, *Ego Is the Enemy* (New York: Portfolio, 2016), 39

87 *"False ideas about yourself"* Ibid.

88 *it has only been slightly improved on* https://www.roadandtrack.com/car-culture/classic-cars/a26081/lost-art-the-english-wheel/

90 *his family was responsible* https://tcowboyarts.org/members/wilson-capron/

90 *The timing and cooperation* http://www.prorodeo.com/prorodeo/rodeo/rodeo101/team-roping

92 *Spurs go back to the time* http://www.cowboyshowcase.com/spurs
.html#.Wqrd_5MbNE4

92 *The rowel spur that we would recognize* Ibid.

93 *Before that, the West was considered* Christopher Knowlton,
Cattle Kingdom: The Hidden History of the Cowboy West
(New York: Eamon Dolan/Houghton Mifflin, 2017) 4

93 *Spurred on by the railroads* https://www.history.com/topics/cowboys

93 *Though they still serve an essential need* Ibid.

95 *Researchers have determined* http://ideas.time.com/2011/11/30
/the-protege-effect/ and https://digest.bps.org.uk/2018/05/04
/learning-by-teaching-others-is-extremely-effective-a-new-
study-tested-a-key-reason-why/

CHAPTER TEN

109 *However, one ingenious doctor* Michael Harris, *The End of
Absence: Reclaiming What We've Lost in a World of Constant
Connection* (New York: Current, 2014), 138–139

CHAPTER ELEVEN

122 *The first mechanical clockmakers* https://www.thoughtco.com
/clock-and-calendar-history-1991475

CHAPTER TWELVE

132 *Germany is a thriving modern* https://www.nytimes.com
/2017/09/21/business/german-election-jobs.html

133 *Close to 60 percent* https://www.theatlantic.com/business
/archive/2014/10/why-germany-is-so-much-better-at-training-
its-workers/381550/

133 *European countries far surpass* https://www.urban.org/urban-
wire/strong-apprenticeship-model-can-help-solve-americas-
workforce-challenges

133 *"it's not unusual to find"* https://www.washingtonpost.com/news
/grade-point/wp/2017/12/22/why-are-apprenticeships-a-good-idea-
that-have-never-really-taken-off-in-the-u-s/

133 *Only around 5 percent*   https://www.theatlantic.com/business
/archive/2014/10/why-germany-is-so-much-better-at-training-
its-workers/381550/

134 *Known as "Queen of the Weapons"*   Knowledge Hub:, Great
Courses Plus: https://www.youtube.com/watch?v=c94vhjGsC8M

135 *"whole cultures grew up"*   http://cashenblades.com/mathertonforge
/index.php/ancient-steel/

136 *the distinctive curved Japanese*   http://www.shadowofleaves.com
/sword-history/

149 *"I hope that there are always"*   Songkeepers, 1999. http://filmcatalog
.nmai.si.edu/title/1545/

Chapter Fourteen

163 *Archeologists have recently*   https://www.smithsonianmag.com
/science-nature/early-bow-and-arrows-offer-insight-into-origins-
of-human-intellect-112922281/

163 *If this is proven to be true*   Ibid.

163 *around 2500 B.C., the Central Asians*   https://quatr.us/africa
/invented-bow-arrow.htm

163 *Native Americans in North America*   https://archaeology.uiowa
.edu/american-indian-archery-technology-0

163 *One advantage is that*   Ibid.

165 *Flint knapping, the process of making*   http://www.cherokeeheritage
.org/attractions/flintknapping/

Chapter Fifteen

173 *Look for the person in the object*   James Krenov, *The Impractical
Cabinetmaker* (Linden Publishing, 1999) 157

179 *"any place producing"*   http://www.dictionary.com

180 *A century and a half later*   https://www.statisticbrain.com
/denim-jeans-industry-statistics/

Chapter Seventeen

200 *Recent archeological evidence* https://www.smithsonianmag.com /history/archaeology-chocolate-180954243/

200 *It was so valued* https://recipes.howstuffworks.com/food-facts /history-of-chocolate1.htm

200 *Later, the Aztecs were* https://www.godivachocolates.co.uk /the-history-of-chocolate-mayans-aztecs.html

200 *In the sixteenth century* https://www.cadbury.com.au/about-chocolate/discovering-chocolate.aspx

200 *The first chocolate bars* https://www.everydayhealth.com /nutrients/calories/delicious-history-candy-bars/

201 *a time-consuming and intensive* https://www.zagat.com /b/8-bean-to-bar-chocolate-makers-to-know

Chapter Eighteen

204 *"their philosophy of living"* Krenov, 10

ABOUT THE AUTHORS

LIKE HIS HOMETOWN of Detroit, **ERIC GORGES**'s story is one of repurposing and rebuilding. After a devastating health crisis in the late 1990s, Eric—a self-confessed IT nerd—walked away from a lucrative corporate career for good. At that period in his life, he knew three very simple things: He loved bikes, he loved working with his hands, and he needed a job. He sought out one of the best metal shapers in the country and eventually signed on as his apprentice. Starting in the business from the ground floor up, Eric started working on vintage cars and motorcycles. In April of 1999 he decided to strike out on his own, building custom motorcycles, and Voodoo Choppers was born. His PBS show, *A Craftsman's Legacy*, began in 2014 and is currently in preproduction on its fifth season.

JON STERNFELD is the coauthor of *A Stone of Hope: A Memoir* with Jim St. Germain, *Strong in the Broken Places: A Memoir of Addiction and Redemption through Wellness* with Quentin Vennie, and *Crisis Point: Why We Must—and How We Can—Overcome Our Broken Politics in Washington and Across America* with Senators Tom Daschle and Trent Lott. He lives in New York.